Resurrection Peacemaking: Plowsharing the Tools of War

Resurrection Peacemaking: Plowsharing the Tools of War

Thirty Years with Christian Peacemaker Teams

CLIFFORD KINDY

RESOURCE *Publications* · Eugene, Oregon

RESURRECTION PEACEMAKING: PLOWSHARING THE TOOLS OF WAR
Thirty Years with Christian Peacemaker Teams

The poem in chapter 9 first appeared in The Mennonite, January, 2003.

Resource Publications
An Imprint of Wipf and Stock Publishers
199 W. 8th Ave., Suite 3
Eugene, OR 97401

www.wipfandstock.com

PAPERBACK ISBN: 978-1-7252-7896-7
HARDCOVER ISBN: 978-1-7252-7897-4
EBOOK ISBN: 978-1-7252-7898-1

Manufactured in the U.S.A.   10/15/20

Contents

Preface

THIS BOOK RELATES STORIES from my time with Christian Peacemaker Teams (CPT) and connects those stories with the collapse of war. Am I serious that the collapse of war is our new reality? If I draw from my personal experience, it is absolutely true. War has the capacity to destroy everything in its path but is impotent to build up society in any way. Yet war remains the default setting in the political arena, since humanity has not chosen to utilize the available tools of nonviolence.

This is where nonviolence comes into play. Nonviolence is most effective when it intentionally retakes the initiative from the actors of violence. Nonviolence is active, not passive. It has the power to rally civil society because its practice makes sense morally. Nonviolent tools are much more effective than the tools of war. That effectiveness, though, does not mean that nonviolent practitioners will not be injured or killed in the struggle.

My understanding of nonviolence is not some rote textbook application. Nonviolence in a setting of injustice emerges from the wisdom of local partners and the advocacy of a partnering group or groups. At its best, nonviolence flowers from the joint willingness of those colleagues to act with flexibility in the face of risk.

Why will people be willing to risk their lives to confront violence or injustice? For me, that willingness is grounded in the gospel story of Jesus' resurrection. For others, it will be based in love and goodness.

Resurrection Peacemaking begins with the drama of Israeli occupation in Gaza. Chapter 2 flies us back to Joyfield Farm in Indiana: what is life like at home for this CPTer? I then discuss the constructive program, an outline that grows a new future. From there we consider where genuine security can be found. Chapter 5 takes us on pilgrimage, a spiritual undergirding for the struggle. The training for a Muslim Peacemaker Team then demonstrates the interfaith nature of nonviolence.

Abruptly, the next two chapters lodge us firmly in Nigeria and the fear and violence of Boko Haram. In Chapter 9, a poem transfers us back through time to the start of the US invasion of Baghdad in 2003. Then a glimpse at values of transparency and accountability prepare us to see the Good Samaritan in the guise of our enemy in Chapter 11.

Great Expectations return us to Iraq to relive that Samaritan gospel story. In Chapter 13, memories linger from the suicide visitors to our home in Baghdad. Then we glimpse the strong links between corporate capitalism and war, before riding into the wild campo of Colombia in Chapter 15.

Do violent actors find value in nonviolence? Chapter 16 answers in the affirmative. Then we live with the nonviolent Las Abejas in Chiapas, Mexico, under extreme injustice, before switching to the Chapter 18 campaign against the US Navy in Vieques, Puerto Rico.

Almost as an aside, Chapter 19 takes us on a flying trip into and out of Israel, exposing the calculated violence that over long decades has held Palestinians in a bondage of injustice. Chapter 20 winds our chapters toward a close with an uncompleted campaign to end the manufacture of depleted uranium weapons, followed by an examination of the alternative to either empire violence or radical resistance violence. We reach the summit of the book in the Democratic Republic of the Congo in Chapter 22, where we meet Pastor Kuye and Sister Maseeka as they retake the initiative from actors of violence.

There are some important appendices. The lead appendix lists some general tools of nonviolence followed by my personal inventory of nonviolent actions, to stimulate readers to shape their own lists. Because war is not the usual mode of living for many of us, Appendix C collects my war blogs from Nigeria depicting the panorama of war's devastation. Appendix D offers brainstorming from the DU campaign to complete the quartet. The book then concludes with a substantial bibliography of further suggested readings for the serious student to consider.

Reader, you are entering a journey. Your world is about to be upended. Hold tightly to your Spirit and be prepared to discover Miracle on your team!

CLIFF KINDY, JUNE 2020

Introduction

A COLLECTION OF GUNS, with a young man loading the bullets and pulling the triggers, killed fifty people and injured fifty more in Christchurch, New Zealand. One wonders if it was fear or self-image that caused the gun manufacturer or the shooter to desire such a result.

Was the manufacturer afraid, or was the young man afraid? Was it fear that caused the operators of the company to sell such a product, to assuage the fear of being poor? Was it the young man's fear that required him to kill people, in this case all of them Muslims? Was he afraid of Muslims? Did killing them end his fear of them or other humans?

Did the killings somehow make him or the gun manufacturer whole? Do human beings need to kill to feel okay in their own bodies? When I need another's death to somehow complete my wholeness, am I missing something? In war, does killing provide a positive future for me? Does the death of another person, or the ability to manipulate a gun in an effective manner, give me personal psychological affirmation?

When two of us from Christian Peacemaker Teams (CPT) joined the village of Rio Nuevo Ité in Colombia, the community had just returned from the mountains in which they had taken refuge from violence. Upon return, the first things the community did were to plant bananas, set the hens to hatch eggs, and clean up the ransacked schoolroom for the children. These actions opened a future for them. These "planting" events provided hope and security for them. These actions plowshared what had been violence and injustice into peace-building events (Isaiah 2:4 and Micah 4:3). Using plowshare as a verb highlights the active nature of this transformational process.

It was an armed incursion into their village that had sent the community fleeing into the mountains for refuge. Those same armed actors, military and paramilitary, were still operating in the region. Yet the community of Rio Nuevo Ité did not feel a need to arm itself to be whole or shield its fear. I suspect the villagers felt some uneasiness, but why did they not feel they needed to obtain guns for safety when the gun manufacturers and young man in New Zealand did?

Alternatively, is it the need to make money that is the driving force in gun manufacture and use? Did the young man somehow gain value by killing people? Do those who encourage war do it for money? Does that justify the action somehow in the minds of politicians? Does our economic system, capitalism, require wars to survive? The push to export weapons for the "good" of the economy would seem to verify that presumption. What if maximizing wealth or economic power were not our society's objectives?

Today, mercenaries—bought gunners and private contractors—are one of the primary sources of US military fighters. If they had other, non-killing options to make a living, would they choose not to join the military? Or are they afraid? Or are they not feeling whole or good in themselves? How do we alleviate that fear without killing others? How can we enable others or ourselves to be whole without resorting to violence?

Clearly killing does not end the fear. If war or massacres ended fear, war and massacres would not be cyclic. They would not need to be repeated.

Let's go deeper.

FOR ME, JESUS' RESURRECTION is the event that ignites the spirit of peace-makers and turns on its head that cycle of fear, wars, and massacres. In Jesus' resurrection from the grave, the powers of death were defeated with nonviolent power. Death was swallowed up (1 Cor 15:54) by the victory of peacemaking power. The defeat of the powers of death are the experiences this book relates. This is resurrection peacemaking in the flesh.

I would term the peacemaking practice that fills this book "theology with feet." My assignments with CPT required me to travel, and specifically to travel into war zones. My theology expected me to put skin in the game. My feet led the way and my body and heart had to follow. When theology is just words, it can be easy to simply hold a belief as a good idea. When theology embodies action—when I put my feet on the ground—there is risk involved.

In New Testament times, the Roman Empire was the power that set up the cross on Golgotha. Rome's soldiers carried out the execution for crimes of treason. The emperor's seal was on the stone that closed the tomb. It was Rome's soldiers that guarded the tomb and then reported the problem of the missing, resurrected body.

Rome was all-powerful militarily, but God acted with a different power that rendered as nothing the might of Rome. Love does that. The God-love that Jesus lived and talked about throughout his life is also what he invited his disciples to model in their living. That love is displayed in the tools of nonviolence, which plowshare the machines of resistance to empire as well as machines of empire. The instruments of love allow all users of tools of violence to concede their weakness without being obliterated.

My experience is that the tools of nonviolence plowshare the tools of war in ways that provide an opening for a future that builds humanity and honors God's good creation. At the same time, the persistence of the equipment of violence, if not replaced by a nonviolent resistance, will continue to destroy humanity and God's creation.

FOR THIRTY YEARS I have been immersed in the work of Christian Peacemaker Teams and similar efforts in many of the war zones of the world. Those journeys were team efforts with CPT in places like Gaza, the West Bank, Chiapas, Iraq, First Nation settings, Colombia, conflict sites here in the United States, the Democratic Republic of the Congo, Nigeria, and Vieques. They were times that we in CPT learned about nonviolence, using old and new instruments of peacemaking.

In 1989, the Church of the Brethren asked me to represent the denomination on the Steering Committee of CPT. At that time, I would have said we were kindergartners in peacemaking. Maybe we have graduated into first or second grade by now. Already though, in nonviolence we have the means to end any war—*if* we are willing to take the risks and utilize our imaginations.

MY FAMILY HAS BEEN an integral part of this committed experiment as disciples following in the steps of Jesus, the Prince of Peace. Arlene and our daughters, Erin and Miriam, have each been volunteers with CPT delegations and teams. They have helped host CPT Congresses, gone on speaking tours, and attended meetings. They also have given me critical encouragement to push ahead on often-long tours away from our home at Joyfield Farm.

My uncles chose varied routes as they faced the selective service draft for wars during their lives. Some had deferments for pastoral ministry or agricultural responsibilities. Others chose to participate in alternative service as conscientious objectors to war. The rest joined different branches of the military. Uncle Don's life may have been the challenge that inspired me to dig most deeply into peacemaking.

Our family often kept track of Uncle Don as I was growing up. He was in the air force, in locations such as Greece and Laos. He was also in Cambodia, where war started shortly after he arrived. When he settled here in the United States, we looked at each other knowingly.

Uncle Don did not single-handedly start that war. But wars are intentional, just as peace is intentional. We make choices with our lives. Our taxes, our words, our way of life, our relationships, our awareness of barriers, our willingness to build them or break them down, our openness to different people, our jobs, our fears, and our hopes: these are all choices that lead toward war or toward peace. This book chronicles my attempt to move toward peace. With it, I invite you, the reader, to make similar choices intentionally, with an understanding of the resurrection power you carry in your body.

I AM OUT FOR my early morning walk, a bit earlier than usual. Arlene is still gone, cooking for the volunteers rebuilding in North Carolina with Brethren Disaster Ministries. I am alone. During my twenty-minute walk along Wabash County Road 1400 North, not a single car passes me, though I spot one set of car lights on a parallel road a mile away. One plane cuts cross-ways through the night sky. I hear a freight train warming the tracks heading west along the rails that pass through Sydney about five miles to the north. I am all alone with the night.

But the sky! The Big Dipper, Ursa Major—Harriet Tubman's guide star through the busy nights on the underground railroad out of slavery—is still marking our route toward the now-melting North Pole. The Dipper is joined this early morning by a billion other lights crowding the sky above my head, especially along the band called the Milky Way, the galaxy in which we on Earth are but a minute part.

Widening our imaginations through these galaxy images may be a helpful mind-expanding exercise as we contemplate the transition, the plowsharing, from violence into nonviolence. [These italicized comments, reflections, and questions will be interspersed throughout the text as further stimulants to your engagement with the issues of this book.]

As I walk, the awesome sky reminds me of Dale Auckerman's comments during a visit with him and his wife Ruth, while he and I were on the Steering Committee of CPT. He was reading and commenting on a passage from Genesis 11—that God looked *down* on the huge tower that humanity had constructed *way up* into the sky.

I suspect God looks down today at our feeble efforts of war and peace. God looks down at our cracking of the atom, our sleuthing in the ocean depths, and our drilling deep under the crust of the Earth's mantle. God looks down at our attempts to understand the human psyche to cure PTSD, frequently caused by our inhumanity to each other. God looks down at this tiny book thrown into the mix of violence and love. How insignificant are humanity's moves upon this planet in the tiny solar system thrown into our one galaxy, which is but a tiny piece of a chaotically patterned universe on a screen where there may be other parallel universes. What is humanity that God should even care a whit? (Psalm 8:4 and Hebrews 2:6)

However, the biblical record is clear: God has immense love for this tiny speck flung through space. God has endless love for this tiny you and tiny me gravitationally glued to this speck. For me, for you, for the entire human race, and all the created world, God throws out a lifeline of love. It is a resurrection love that we are invited to emulate in our interactions with others. It is a love from which we are seemingly unable to extract ourselves in the grand scheme of creation. That resurrection makes possible any task of plowsharing we may contemplate.

This book attempts to highlight the route we can trek along the star paths to disentangle humanity from the web of fear. Nonviolence is rooted in the love of God for the world and each human being. I see that resurrection love-power most clearly in Jesus, so I try to disciple my living after his life.

TODAY SEBASTIÁN AND LEONARDO, two of our grandsons, aged nine and five, are joining me here at Joyfield Farm for the day. What kind of world are we leaving for them? What if those of us on this globe choose to work together to tackle the issues that threaten any future, instead of warring together and destroying any possibility of a future? Are we leaving in their hands the tools to build peace, the framework of a constructive program from which they can shape life into the future?

These two boys are cross cultural. Sebas started with three languages, his dad's native Q'eqchi', his parents' common Spanish, and the English of the society in which they are being raised. They have a head start on breaking down barriers. They are inquisitive and ready to take risks. Perhaps the record contained in this book will serve as a step stool to move up to the next phase beyond ending war—toward building a future of ecological balance, of racial equality, of economic justice. Blessings of peace for the journey, Grandsons!

A journey is a pilgrimage, often in a direction where there are many unknowns. It can be a vulnerable act of faith because of risks that might make the way dangerous or difficult. A pilgrimage involves steps or movements toward an anticipated goal. Some steps may be on paths already traversed that seem to indicate possibilities toward goodness. Other steps may venture in new directions with just a gleaming hint of a new and better future. Both have value.

I offer this book as a series of stories and reflections that grapple with humanity's urgent search for peace in a world where war is the default action in the face of violence, injustice, or economic slowdown. It is a very personal account of my own life, shared with the trust that readers will weave in their own stories and thus become players in the drama. Together we will be part of the generation that ends war and builds a new future. The tools for plowsharing into that future are at hand. We need only to boldly enter risky fields of conflict and injustice with the expectation that our own hands and spirits really do hold the tools that make for peace.

Chapter 1

Gaza Night

IN THE SUMMER OF 1993, Gene Stoltzfus, the first director of Christian Peacemaker Teams, approached me. He said, "Cliff, we think you should be part of the team that goes to the Gaza Strip." My family and I talked about this request, and then responded that since our two daughters were still young and I felt responsible for them, I'd better not go.

At the time, I was a member of the Steering Committee of Christian Peacemaker Teams. CPT had sent short delegations to Palestine and other hot spots, but this would be the first team sent for a longer time.

Gene asked again. The team would be going July, August, and September, the busiest time for our market garden, our primary income source. We felt I couldn't leave all that work for Arlene and the girls and told Gene so.

Gene asked again. He was persistent. Miriam, 12 years old at the time, said, "Daddy, many fathers and sons leave home in Gaza and never return, but you will only be gone for three months. Maybe we should make it possible for you to go."

Daddy went.

RABBI JEREMY MILGROM MET the CPT team in Jerusalem to prepare us for the trip to Gaza. He said to us, "When you cross the borders into Gaza, you cross the borders into hell." We were a team of four that finally entered Gaza: Elayne McClannen from Carlisle, Pennsylvania; Phyllis Butt from Louisville, Ohio; David Weaver from Hartville, Ohio; and I from North

Manchester, Indiana. Duane Ediger, our fifth team member, was refused entry at Tel Aviv because he had been arrested for crossing the so-called Green Line between Israel and Palestine a year earlier.

According to the United Nations, Gaza was the most densely populated area in the world. Unemployment was over 80% since Israel had closed its borders. Gaza's Palestinian workers employed in agriculture and construction jobs in Israel could no longer get out to their work. Schools, kindergarten through university, had been shut down by the Israeli occupation for four years.

Giardia was in the water supply. Public water also had 400 parts per million nitrates and 600 parts per million chlorides. A two-liter pop bottle of tap water placed on the counter overnight settled out a milky fluid in the bottom half. There was no sewage system; I would straddle an open ditch as I walked the narrow alleys, my backpack nearly hitting the homes at each shoulder. There was no garbage pickup either, so shepherd boys grazed their flocks on the trash that blew and collected into drifts.

The Palestinian Center for Human Rights (PCHR) office in Gaza City, under the strong leadership of Raji Sourani, had invited Christian Peacemaker Teams to send a team. This was a trial run for CPT: would it help reduce the violence to have an international peacemaking presence in a conflict zone? This would be the first permanent team CPT sent into a conflict zone. Team members were to stay in the homes of refugee families—a different family each week.

The second week Islamic Jihad scrawled a message on a wall, reading, "All North Americans should be either kidnapped or killed." This was a bit sobering, so our team examined the options. With the promise of support from PCHR, we finally decided to stay.

About the third or fourth week I was headed to Rafah Refugee Camp, on the border with Egypt. As we got close to the camp, we were met at an Israeli checkpoint. A soldier poked his gun in the front window of the car and said, "Let's see an ID." He waved us on in, and I could see bigger Israeli guns up an embankment above us.

As we drove into the Shaburra section of the camp, we entered a vast open space where Palestinian homes had been demolished by Israeli bulldozers. Israeli military forces were on the roof of a tall two-story building. With the sweep of guns they patrolled the area within their view, an area where children played. I could hear gunshots in the distance. Occasionally jeeps raced up, squealed to a stop, and soldiers jumped out with guns at the ready. We had entered a war zone.

That afternoon my host accompanied me to a wake. A day earlier Israeli soldiers were pursuing a young Palestinian man. He could be wanted for some infraction at a checkpoint or for being from the wrong political party. His younger brother stepped in front of the pursuing soldiers and took seven shots below his waist. Rafah, despite a population of two hundred thousand, had no hospital. So medical personnel took him to Khan Younis, a nearby city. There he died in the hospital when Israeli soldiers refused to allow the doctors to enter. We were at his wake. Even with tight checkpoints on the streets, and soldiers on rooftops around the wake site, about two thousand people attended.

Mid-afternoon, his family asked me through an interpreter if I would be willing to stay with them through the night. Soldiers had raided the home the night before, ransacking each room in the house, shooting out the only shower and sink in the house, shooting holes through the metal roof, and stomping on the hands of a baby sleeping on the floor as they departed. The family was afraid they might return and wanted me to stay with them.

I am an organic market gardener in Indiana. I use wheelbarrows and shovels; we don't have guns in our home. Quickly in my mind I pondered, *Well, Cliff, why did you come?*

"Okay," I said, "I will stay with you."

At 9 p.m., the nightly curfew started and thirteen of us filed into the home. We ate supper. Well, three of us did, two of the family and the guest. I don't speak Arabic and they didn't speak English, but we could exchange names and I could learn some new words. I could sense the tension in the air.

At midnight there was a knock on the door. It got more insistent, a gun butt beating against the door. The sister, who became the presence of the Spirit for me that night, went to answer. Seven Israeli soldiers barged in, knowing exactly what was to happen that night and how it was going to happen. Then they noticed me sitting against the wall in my pajamas and sandals, heart pounding in my chest. They didn't know who I was, but it was clear that I wasn't from Rafah Camp!

They hesitated then proceeded politely through each room of the house, trying to regain control of the situation. On the way out they seized the two older brothers. The sister made it very clear to me that if anything was to occur, it would be outside—and if I wanted to be present, I'd better get outside.

The squad was asking the brothers to take down the posters of Muneer, the brother who had been killed. They also asked the brothers to take down the tarp that had shaded the wake area and to whitewash the walls. The walls served as a newspaper since no newspaper was allowed to be printed in Gaza. The brothers did take down the tarp but refused to do the other tasks.

I had tried earlier to speak with the soldiers, but they indicated they spoke no English and I didn't speak Hebrew either. Ariel, whose name I understood means lion, was the captain of the squad. He was the type of person who makes lists and crosses off tasks as the jobs get done.

Things weren't happening very fast and there apparently was still lots to do this night. Ariel played the point of his gun across my chest and asked, "Cliff, why don't you take down the posters?"

I had heard of reflective listening, so I responded, "It's very important for you that the posters come down, right, Ariel?"

"Yes, Cliff."

"And you want me to take them down?"

"Yes, Cliff."

But I didn't know where to go next with reflective listening. I was not looking forward to spending the night on the streets of Rafah Camp if I took the signs down after the brothers had refused to do so. On the other hand, I didn't relish the alternative of not even needing a place to stay that night! I was saved from my dilemma when four more soldiers came in off the street, for no one could speak English anymore and each had to be more macho than the others.

Soon some soldiers knocked on a neighbor's door. There was no answer and I could hear the door splinter beneath the gun butts. Five "volunteers" were brought out to speed the work.

"Do you know the writings of Mark Twain? Remember when Tom Sawyer was asked by his aunt to whitewash the walls? Tonight's activities remind me of that story, but tonight's story has a strange twist," I injected into this madness.

Ariel immediately confronted me, "Who are you, Cliff? Where are you from?"

"I'm from Indiana."

"Why are you here?"

"I guess I'm here because I have the hope that in situations of conflict we can learn how to live with each other without resorting to guns, stacking up the bodies, and the tallest stack wins."

"Living without guns will never happen here, Cliff."

"But remember when the Hebrews were slaves in Egypt, God intervened there."

"God will never intervene here."

Ariel, the task-oriented man, was running out of time and tasks were uncompleted. He began to back the brothers up against the wall with his weapon. I felt I was in a room flooded with gasoline with someone about to drop a flaming match into the fuel. I stepped between the gun and the brothers.

Just then a bird flew overhead. "What is that bird?"

"That is a monkey-faced owl."

"We don't have anything like that in Indiana." It was a dark owl with white under markings on a moonlit night, beautiful for anything except what was happening. Then the mate flew in and the two owls circled above our heads. It was as though an arm reached out and pulled us back from the edge of the abyss.

Shortly after, the soldiers left. Through an interpreter the next day, the mother told me, "A miracle happened last night." I was clear that a miracle had happened, but for me it was not just her awe that no one was arrested, the home was not trashed again, and no one else was killed.

The miracle I finally understood was that God does not need us to have all the skills, speak all the right languages, and be filled with nonviolent expertise. God just wants us to be available. If we are available, God will work the miracles of peacemaking.

Chapter 2

Growing Peace with Hoosier Roots

ARLENE AND I OFTEN comment to ourselves that the most important peace-making work we do is here at Joyfield Farm in Indiana where we live. Here we try to develop a lifestyle that is both sustainable and just in a world where unsustainability and injustice run rampant. Joyfield Farm has been our home from 1983 until the present.

When we married in 1971, Arlene and I made the commitment to keep our income below the federal taxable level so we would not be paying taxes for war. Because we saw war as a dead-end game for all involved, we did not want to encourage war by paying for it. We have been able to keep that covenant.

For the years of our marriage, the US federal discretionary budget has consistently designated fifty percent or more for military purposes. Some war supporters could choose to pay extra to grow war, but I have never heard of such a deed. Some pay only a symbolic portion and write a letter to explain their tax resistance. Others refuse to pay the entire military portion and send it to an escrow account or to an organization working for peace and justice. We have intended not to pay for war because we follow the Prince of Peace. We also choose to live a lifestyle that doesn't need so much to be defended by war.

Although some object that living on that income level is impossible in today's world, Arlene and I have gone to school paying our own way. We have raised a family, hopefully without chasing our children into the pursuit of money and material things. We bought seven acres of land with another family, Bob and Rachel Gross, with both families living under the taxable income level. We built a house, albeit transformed from a corncrib—well insulated, with field stone on the outside, nestled among trees we planted. We have a market garden business that seems to thrive, except for one severe drought year.

Someone asked daughter Miriam one time, "What is it like to grow up poor?"

"Poor?!" she exclaimed, "We are among the richest people in the world. We eat food that the richest people can only dream of. We travel the world with disaster and peace building efforts. The world passes through our home with visitors from across the globe. Our home is tight, easy to heat, easily cleaned, spacious for lots of guests and beautiful in a setting of trees, flowers, and birds. I did not grow up poor!"

Sweat equity replaced the shortage of cash. We asked friends if they would loan us money for the initial purchase of the land and rundown buildings, which they did. We paid them back in a few short years. The farmhouse where we first lived needed a new roof and chimney before winter, so we did those repairs.

A standing seam metal roof will last one hundred years with care, so we were determined to do that. I had worked with an older carpenter in Ohio when we ripped off a standing seam roof to replace it with a new shingle roof. He explained to me that the already seventy-five-year-old standing seam roof would have outlasted the new shingle roof we were nailing on.

We could not afford to pay workers to do the standing seam roof job on our large farmhouse. So, I asked the nearby Bolinger Tin Shop if I could work with one of them on our house one morning to learn the techniques. We would then purchase the materials from them and rent the special tools that go with this trade. They agreed, and thirty-seven years later the roof remains.

My father was a pastor, so I didn't grow up comfortable with carpentry, though Mom's father had been a carpenter after his years of mining coal. I remember playing in the wood shavings of the shop near Grandpa and Grandma Zimmerman's old farmhouse. I learned carpentry though by doing volunteer disaster relief work. I spent my first six months in Brethren Volunteer Service cleaning up and rebuilding after Hurricane Camille in Mississippi. That was followed by well over fifty other volunteer stints with Brethren Disaster Ministries where our family worked with some of the best carpenters and builders from across the country. They often did the tasks differently but that meant I could choose the techniques that best suited me.

Our daughters would regularly travel with Arlene and me as we rebuilt after floods, tornadoes, and hurricanes. They were not with us when we responded to wars, earthquakes, and tsunamis. But they learned from Mom and Dad. They were in their early and mid-teens when they and Arlene volunteered in Puerto Rico after one of the recurrent hurricanes there. Other young volunteer men asked our daughters, "What are girls going to be able to do here?"

"Would you like us to lay up the corners of the block walls so you can run the courses of block in between, or mark out the roof so you can nail down shingles?" Erin responded, and effectively shut down their incredulity.

We were not trained as market gardeners either, though Arlene did grow up on a dairy farm. Both our families did care for gardens to be able to eat fresh produce, and to then freeze and can food for the winter. Making an income from the garden fell into our lap in a way. The first year we lived in the farmhouse and had a garden just east of the homestead, south of the pear trees. We had extra at the end of the season and put a sign out by the road. We sold about $150 of produce.

We expanded our garden when Bob and Rachel moved into the farmhouse with us, after they had finished their work in Philadelphia with death penalty abolition efforts. They had two daughters as well, of similar ages to our girls. That youthful energy soon swelled the seams of the farmhouse so we spent a year making a home of the old corncrib. We also worked up more land for gardening, and the second year we sold $300 at the roadside.

Income from the garden kept doubling each year until we asked ourselves whether we could in fact live from the income of a larger market garden. We joined in an effort to develop a farmers' market in North Manchester. Later I served as the market master, a kind of facilitator of the vendors—arranging advertising, growing the number of vendors, and supporting the Women Infant Children (WIC) program providing healthy food for mothers, babies, and young children. The garden has now been our primary income for over twenty-five years.

We homeschooled Erin and Miriam all but four years, combined, of their primary and high school careers. The disaster stints and the regular activities with the garden were frequent segments of the school curriculum. The reader might expect that such routines would chase young children far from any garden activity when it became their choice. No, both have families with adequate gardens to feed hungry mouths, store food for winter, and school young hands and minds for the next generation!

As a family we have lived on $6,000–12,000 each year. It has been more than sufficient. We are probably still in the upper five percent of the world's population by income. What style of living is at a level that the world could environmentally sustain for the entire world population? What level of living does not need to be defended by war? How will we choose to use limited resources? If we counted the cleanup and repair costs for damage done by a practice or tool of violence, what would be the real cost?

If, for example, we had to pay for the cleanup and health costs of depleted uranium weapons, would anyone be able to afford them? Only when those costs can be passed on to unsuspecting civilians as collateral health catastrophes, or deferred to an unborn generation, can people even think about using such tools!

What if the costs in health, resource replacement, and carbon cleanup were included in the purchase price of an automobile? That would make a more realistic choice for us as we ponder what kind of vehicle we will use. It was good for us as a family to not have a car for the first twelve years of our married life. I still ride a bicycle the seven miles to church on occasion, and I have taken a cart behind my bicycle to go to the smaller Wednesday market with produce. It is not always convenient because of rain or too much produce, but it may be the more sustainable choice.

What about elevators? For some folks they are a necessity to get to other levels in a building. Most of us, though, are able to walk up the few flights of stairs that elevators carry us. What about house size? How large a building do we need to live in? Are the piles of stuff we buy, and then store in closets and storage warehouses, necessary? What happens when we run out of resources? Or space to dump our waste? Every item we have and every process we pursue as part of our living merits a close examination in light of justice to the environment and its people. It is possible to think ahead and begin the steps of doing with less.

Another way to think about the issues is to ask, "Does my living require a war to defend it?" Mahatma Gandhi said something like, "If I have more than I need when another has less than s/he needs, I am a thief." Can we live with open hands and hearts, without locks and walls? Can we live as sharing, caring people instead of driving Abrams tanks or strapping explosives to our bodies? If we had fewer of the world's resources here in the United States, it would make war machinery less important. We would not need that machinery to maintain those resources just for us.

For twenty years Arlene and I have been receiving requests from younger and older people asking if they can intern with us. We usually ask what they mean by that: "What would you like to do here? How can we help with that? What ways can we together grapple with questions that to this point do not have answers?"

So, often other people live with us. They live in one of the upstairs bedrooms and take their meals with us. Sometimes they eat differently than we do so it means adjustments for us and them. They usually have other ways to do the things we do at home and in the garden, so it forces us to be flexible and I'm sure does the same for them.

"Teach us how to grow food." Well, we do that here at Joyfield Farm, so we can show how we do it. But in another location, with different climate or soil, you may have to develop a uniquely different way.

As I write, I think of folks who have been here with us, who are now living in at least eight different states and another country. Maybe we grow interns too!

WHEN I WENT WITH CPT to Iraq in 2002, we decided that we needed to figure how to use less petroleum so that we would not be going to war for oil. I stopped using a gasoline (or any fuel) garden tiller. I just started using a hoe to till the soil. It worked well for fourteen years. Then, friends suggested an even lower tillage style that we have been using in recent years. We keep asking how long we can maintain this physically intense type of gardening. Maybe it keeps us healthy? It certainly gets me in shape each spring!

The soil on our land is a sandy loam. In drought years, the fields around here would not make much of a harvest, so there are four large center pivot irrigation systems within a mile of our place. Watering crops is nice, but if the aquifer runs dry in a few decades—as the Ogallala Aquifer under Kansas, Nebraska, and Oklahoma appears destined to do in a few years—then what? How will we grow food then?

So, Arlene and I decided to try other techniques. We compost most everything and have eight huge compost piles around the garden. This way, lots of humus—decayed plants and animal manure—ends up back in the garden each year. We have a permanent mulch of straw or leaves between the rows. Both mulching and composting practices help hold the moisture we receive. We also plant a cover crop when we take off a garden crop. For instance, when we finish cutting lettuce, we plant the row to a cover crop of soybeans and oats. The soybeans add nitrogen to the soil; the oats provide a cover against rain and wind erosion and add more humus to the soil. Humus holds moisture. Even in our second worst drought year, the garden produced well without drawing water from the well to water it.

What does this have to do with peace? Everywhere I work with CPT, water is one of the issues over which wars are being fought. Here in the United States we already are scrapping between states for water rights, and the countries across our borders are already vying with us for rich water resources. Other distant countries want to bottle the Great Lakes for their use and sale. Water is one of our most important resources, a fact we may discover when California dries up, the Ogallala Aquifer pumps dry, and long-term drought hits the Midwest.

In Israel/Palestine, the occupying country uses over seventy percent of the other country's water. Israel also controls all the wells in the Palestinian West Bank and prevents the installation of water catchment systems by Palestinian farmers and vineyardists. It is said that Israel has made the desert bloom, but it happened at the expense of their neighbors, the Palestinians.

In Iraq, the Tigris and Euphrates River valleys are the cradle of civilization. But the headwaters of both are in Turkey and the Euphrates passes through Syria. When enough dams are built, or water is used—as with the Colorado passing from the United States into Mexico—the two rivers of the cradle of civilization will reach the Persian Gulf as a dribble. Those Iraqi rivers were carefully utilized in times past when the used irrigation water flowed into its own channel so it would not salinate the fresh waters. But those systems were destroyed by the wars. The rivers are severely polluted. The salination is no longer restricted, the same problem faced in much of the Central Valley of California.

These examples mirror many other places around the globe, such as Chiapas, Mexico, Nigeria, Colombia, and China. Learning how to use water is a peace project.

Here at Joyfield Farm, we catch rainwater from the barn and house roofs. We share one well and one water filter for two to four families living on the farm. The filter is needed because the water in our well has high nitrates from traditional farming practices. That is true not only here in Wabash County, but all the way north to the Michigan state line, so we need to filter it to make it safe to drink.

In our stone house we use a composting toilet. It uses no water to flush so saves as much as one hundred gallons of drinking quality water each day. As a society we could easily be utilizing and experimenting with different ways to preserve the resources of our world.

Our compost procedures and cover cropping add sufficient nitrogen and soil nutrients, so we do not add chemical fertilizers or drill in anhydrous ammonia for nitrogen as the farms around us do. Excess nitrogen, and nitrogen that is not accessible to the corn and soybeans planted into fields around us, end up in our well water and in river waters. Downstream, that nitrogen forms huge dead algae fields in the Gulf of Mexico and algal blooms in Lake Erie. Sustainable choices in this arena are steps toward a genuine peace with the environment.

AT JOYFIELD FARM WE have made choices for renewable energy. Early on, our family chose to have a wringer washer and clotheslines to dry clothes outside. Water gets reused many times before going down the drain. There have been three sets of clothes lines here that four families could use. Even in winter, that can suffice or be supplemented by clothes racks that we set up inside, adding moisture to dry living spaces. Renewable solar and wind energy dries our clothes.

We built solar water heaters. Simple sheets of plywood, with one-inch by three-inch board sides, are painted black with a heat-trapping cover over a black garden hose wrapped back and forth. This worked for our family for over twenty-five years to provide our hot water in the summer. The lower end of the hose is connected to the well, and the upper end is connected to a hot water holding tank. The heavier cold water pushes the hot water up into the holding tank. In the winter we do a similar pattern of copper lines around the sides of our wood stove. The stove provides the only heat for our home in winter, other than the large south facing windows on our stone house.

We also built solar cookers. Ours was a science project in home school. Rice cooks nicely in that sun cooker.

Ten years ago, we attached photovoltaic solar panels to our barn roof for producing electricity. Since we are on REMC (Rural Electric Membership Cooperative) lines instead of a private company, the returns are not very economically beneficial for us. Yet, we have been a model for others to install similar systems, and their installations (usually with public utilities) provide a much better return for the initial investment. We have produced enough electricity with thirty-six panels to essentially provide for three households here. We draw from REMC at night and some very cloudy days, but pump extra into the REMC lines on sunny days. That surplus is used by REMC at their peak demand times and we draw back from them at their lowest demand times, so it is a very good deal for REMC. For us, that solar connection has allowed only using batteries the last three years to mow the lawn and, just now, to pump extra electricity into a hybrid plug-in automobile.

The United States economy has been shaped for size and high investment return by large companies. Our experiments here at Joyfield Farm in power, food production, housing, shared economy, and joint effort would appear to match or exceed those mega-efforts when compared with similar investments and accounting for long term costs. While it doesn't make lots of money for a few people at the expense of many others, it works very sustainably. It moves at least in the direction of justice for people and the Earth, while our US economy powers injustice and environmental devastation.

Here at Joyfield Farm we share the purchase costs and upkeep for tools like mowers, chainsaws, water filter, driveway gravel, and the land. When we built our family homes, we at a minimum shared the workloads, and often some of the costs. We divide mowing chores for common areas and share the repair efforts and costs on the large barn we use. Of course, the land costs originally were shared by two families, and at times four families shared the yearly property taxes in a proportional fashion.

These practices may be unusual in our society but are much more common in other societies where family, tribe, or clan are the uniting glue. For the promotion of peace, we have found this shared life is a good building block for strong relationships.

This sharing also provides us the opportunity to cover for each other. Always someone is here to water the plants and to feed the fires in as many as three homes in winter. Always someone is here to feed and water the chickens and gather the eggs. This allows folks to leave to do the work for peace, service, justice, and environment in which all of us find ourselves invested.

Society as a whole seems to be easily distracted by full time jobs, individual efforts, and competition with others. Living arrangements that minimize those attentions facilitate building a more peaceful and sustainable world.

MAKING DO WITH USED items or using damaged or dated foods can be a way to live more sustainably. Some of our building materials were salvaged from buildings that have been torn down. We try to use the produce that may not be so beautiful or has gotten damaged in harvest. We buy clothing from thrift or secondhand stores or use clothing that we make, or others are tossing away.

Many of our necessary food purchases are from bulk food stores and discount groceries where we may use dated foods. Early on we would save good food tossed into dumpsters behind grocery stores. Presently much of our excess garden produce goes to food pantries or soup suppers in the nearby towns of North Manchester and South Whitley. Buying a used car, or just having a used pickup instead of two vehicles, has made good sense for our family for many years.

Eating lower on the food chain has been important for us. Using meats for protein source entails a much higher use of vegetable protein to convert to a usable meat protein. Beef, at a rate of eight to ten units of vegetable protein to produce one unit of meat protein, and hogs, at a six-to-one conversion rate, may not make sense in a sustainable world. Pasture-fed beef can lower that ratio compared to corn-fed beef, and the same is likely true for hogs. Rabbits and chickens or other poultry have a lower conversion rate, nearly three-to-one. Fish is better also. One of these days, grasshoppers and other insects may become prominent protein sources in our sustainable diets.

We have chosen to obtain our protein from vegetables like beans or peanuts, eggs, milk products, nuts, and sometimes fish. Even collards are surprisingly high in protein. Complementary proteins such as bread and peanut butter, beans and rice, pasta and cheese, cereal and milk, or beans and tortillas each provide a complete source of amino acids, the building blocks of proteins. Note that different cultures have self-selected traditional foods with full proteins that don't require huge amounts of water, feed, mechanization, and energy to provide sufficient food for that portion of humanity. Being intentional about how we eat can help us share a world that at this point is still able to provide sufficient food for all of us if we are willing to share and distribute it equitably.

Our family eats a high percentage of its food from local sources—primarily the garden behind our house! Eating more seasonally means we do have a variety of foods. We grow about sixty different kinds of fruits and vegetables which we eat fresh, but for winter meals we do rely more on freezing, canning, storing, and drying to preserve foods.

The usual source of food in our society is a grocery store. Those foods do not have the freshness and nutrition of a backyard garden. They may have traveled hundreds or thousands of miles to reach our table. We won't be able to ascertain with as much confidence how that food was grown, the working conditions of those who cared for its growing, and how safe it is to eat. Local farmers' markets provide a nice compromise that moves us toward justice and environmental sustainability.

Yes, corn-fed beef from Nebraska may also come with a high demand for water. Imported foods like cocoa may rely on slave labor in Sierra Leone. Export crops take land from local farmers in Guatemala so that prime land can grow crops to send to Europe and North America. Growing food for fuel or animals instead of humans may be choices driving us away from peace, away from an environmentally viable world that still meets the needs of all the world's people.

Joyfield Farm is an example of a constructive program that shapes a positive future, plowsharing what has been run down and used up. This plowsharing method holds true in justice-making and peacemaking.

Chapter 3

Constructive Program

Badsha Khan was a Muslim colleague of Mahatma Gandhi's. Gandhi called him the best example of a nonviolent warrior. He grew up in a warrior tribe but early in his life, in 1928, he was attracted to the nonviolence of Gandhi. Khan's charisma and discipline inspired about 100,000 others from the region in what was then North India, today the rugged area on the border of Pakistan and Afghanistan. Khan's group formed the largest nonviolent army the world has seen.

The British feared this disciplined nonviolence so much that they had more troops in this small region than they did in the rest of India to counter, unsuccessfully, Gandhi's nonviolent uprising against the British Crown. Khan spent about half of his life in prison because of his nonviolent civilly disobedient actions striving for freedom from the British occupation.

What he and Gandhi called "the constructive program" was what I can term "retaking the initiative from the actors of violence." It was grounded for both Gandhi and Khan in a deep spirituality, Hinduism and Islam respectively, that carried them through impossible challenges.

For Badsha Khan this constructive program included a disciplined cleanliness of home and village that built self-respect and hygiene. It expanded to incorporate prominent roles for women in a culture that had little honor for women. For him, the education of women and men was an important aspect of strengthening society. The teaching and learning of skills provided a strong economic base enabling the people to stand on their own, independent of the British economic colonialism. Those skills built the foundation for independence even before it was an accomplished fact. The nurturing of unarmed courage in the face of danger and risk overcame the cultural custom of revenge feuds. It then presented a boldness that unnerved the British troops, who had no experience with a strength that refused to do violence to protect itself.

That story is told by Eknath Easwaran in the book, *A Man to Match His Mountains: Badsha Khan, Nonviolent Soldier of Islam*, published by Nilgiri Press. It may be the most dramatic nonviolent story, yet it is almost invisible in the bibliographies of peace and nonviolence. When CPT was in Gaza and Iraq, we passed this book out to folks as an encouragement to Muslim peace workers.

A constructive program is the plan or the steps taken to resist, repair, or replace what is not wanted. It is framed with an objective or later goal in mind.

When we moved to Joyfield Farm in 1983, there was an abundance of trash scattered all around the many buildings and on the land surrounding the buildings. Every time we would walk outside, we would carry containers into which we could gather broken glass, rusty metal pieces from equipment, plastic bags, and aluminum pull tabs. Picking up the trash was a step in improving the appearance of the farm and making the land usable.

Many of the buildings were dilapidated. Building a new chimney and replacing the roof of the farmhouse gave us a warm dry place to live. Building barn doors and replacing missing corner posts secured the barn for our use.

Starting compost piles and setting a plan for enriching the soil helped renew the earth which was quite depleted from years of heavy use. Then planting flowers and trees began the slow process of transforming the appearance of the place and making it inviting to visitors and passersby. Each of these steps at the farm were small pieces of what we could term the constructive program at Joyfield Farm.

In a similar fashion we could imagine a constructive program in a setting of violence or injustice. It might start with public protests against some sexual, racial, or group violence or grievance. Including the aggrieved parties among the protesters affirms the recognition of the wrong done and empowers their own action of change. Then steps of accompaniment, or sessions of training for the group faced with violence, can help strengthen their resolve for a change away from the violence. Making the violence visible in the media might bring allies into the effort to change the injustice.

Enabling economic skills may provide a new self-image that relieves the negative pressure of violence or transforms the earlier relationships.

The goal in these constructive programs is to transform a situation of violence or injustice. The goal is to empower individuals who have been treated wrongly or placed in an inferior role. It enables them to act on their own behalf and find allies for that effort. It takes violating power away from those who have done the violence or injustice but in a way that allows them to hang onto their self-worth. Constructive programs want each person or group to be themselves without destroying or harming others. It replaces something that is unjust with a new, just reality.

Chapter 4

Security

ONE AFTERNOON ON THE streets of Baghdad, around the spring of 2005, a CPT colleague and I met a man who proudly displayed his roll of $100 bills. For every target he reported to US security, he was gifted with $100. So, one might imagine, any antagonist or neighbor toward whom he held a grudge easily became a reported enemy target. Acts of revenge were handed over to US gunners. Lots of folks who had no connection with the resistance became the victims of US counterterrorism. Do similar reports for potential targets service the aerial and drone attacks in Afghanistan and Pakistan? And Yemen and Somalia?

The largest questionable assumption in today's world is that military weapons and tools (the more technological and deadly the better) to counter the "enemy" are the best security one can access to face the fear of terror attacks by "others." So, extraordinary rendition, kidnappings, drones, improvised explosive devices (IEDs), assassinations, torture, varied nuclear capabilities, suicide bombs, mercenary fighters, fighter jets, tanks, resistance units, aircraft carriers, and special forces become the collective operation against the powers that stand in opposition to us and our desires for the world.

Interestingly, the common feature of these security tools is deniability and impunity. The use of these tools is not connected at all with accountability. No one is responsible; no entity has oversight for these operations; no person or political collective can be charged with war crimes. Collateral damage is accidental innocence. The only possible response seems to be to throw more of the security tools used by our side at the other, the "enemy." For example, the use of US drones against Taliban targets in Pakistan invites the response of kidnappings and suicide bombers. The use of kidnappings and suicide bombers against US allies increases the use of drones and special forces operations into Pakistan and threatens the use of major and overt US land attacks in contradiction to Pakistan's sovereignty.

What happens when other countries and even our enemies begin to use drones against human targets in our country or our people in other countries? Those who operate the computer screens for drones in safe locations in Nevada, Wisconsin, Indiana, or elsewhere, and their commanders who give the clearance for a missile strike from the drones, are not held accountable for collateral damage, the killing of innocent civilians. In the same way, suicide bombers have impunity for their attacks on civilians, unless their simultaneous deaths are their unfortunate accountability in a macabre way. Maybe the high suicide rate among those who operate the drones in secure offices scattered presently across the US offers its own unfortunate accountability.

In Iraq during 2004, house raids against Iraqi families became the tool of choice to counter the increasing attacks against US forces. As CPT monitored human rights violations against Iraqi civilians, the common feature of the stories from families was a violent, humiliating invasion of their home in the middle of the night. As this house raid practice became routine in rural, village, and city locations across Iraq, the resistance against the US invasion became almost total.

Right after the US invasion in March 2003, Iraqis would say to CPT, "We may not approve of how it took place, but we are glad Saddam Hussein is gone." Then as time passed, they would say, "Saddam and Bush are brothers. What we had under Saddam we now have under Bush." Then after the attack on the Shiite shrine in Samara in February 2005, "What we now have under Bush is worse than what we experienced under Saddam."

So, if these tools of violence do not provide security, where might we find security? What are possible answers to the question? Fear seems to undergird the lack of security we feel in uncertain situations. What transforms that fear?

Chapter 5

Spirituality in Midwest Pilgrimage

IN DECEMBER 2001, GENE Stoltzfus, Director of Christian Peacemaker Teams (CPT), and Doug Pritchard, CPT Canada director, traveled to Afghanistan to explore placing a CPT team on the ground in that country. The United States had just initiated its military response to the attack on the World Trade Center and Afghanistan was the target.

To undergird Gene and Doug's trip, I proposed a walk from Goshen, Indiana, to Columbus, Ohio, with stops to speak along the route. Seventeen people gathered at Goshen College campus for an anointing and commissioning sendoff. Seven people began walking with me as a symbol of support and encouragement. Arlene, my wife, and Miriam, our younger daughter, took turns driving the support vehicle and walking with me. Erin, our older daughter, was by now working full-time with CPT in Mexico and Colombia.

On the second day of walking, we reached Churubusco where we had made plans to speak and spend the night at the United Methodist Church on the edge of town. At the north edge of town, a police officer pulled off the road to check out "if we were drunk or terrorist." We must have been reassuring since he didn't even check an ID.

Our friend, Lorele Yager, was on the staff at the United Methodist church and took a call from one of the parishioners later in the day. The woman's son, Rick Clevinger, the commanding officer of the Air National Guard Base in Fort Wayne, had called to warn her about a "terrorist" who was walking across Indiana. The parishioner relayed that concern to Lorele and wanted to be sure he wouldn't stay in their church building.

Lorele assured the woman that she knew me well and asked if it might be possible to talk directly with the commander. The mother gave Lorele her son's phone number and Lorele was soon on the phone with the commander. She hoped she could get the commander to talk directly with me, but he was unwilling and continued to voice his concern.

Commander Rick contended that "they" sneak onto bases under false pretenses. "They" poured blood on an airplane. "They" attacked anti-abortionists. "They" entered military bases in New York. In fact, I have entered military bases, but I am pretty clear about why I am there. I have never poured blood on an airplane. I wouldn't call myself pro-abortion and would have no reason to attack anti-abortionists. I have never been to military bases in New York.

My willingness to be vulnerable is a key ingredient to genuine peacemaking. That vulnerability may come in the form of exposure to physical risks against my life, the danger that others may see me or think of me in ways that are inaccurate, or simply that there may be many unknowns in my peacemaking ventures.

Our family did hold a meeting about CPT and did spend the night at the United Methodist Church without incident. We walked the next day into Fort Wayne in time to gather for the late Christmas Eve service at the Beacon Heights Church of the Brethren. I was unexpectedly granted a space to share about my pilgrimage for peace. My support drivers changed that night, with Dean Kindy, my father and longtime pastor, taking the baton from Arlene and Miriam.

June Kindy, my mother, was to join us the next day, so Dad and I took two signs with us to the Air National Guard Base on Christmas Day. This base was sometimes called upon to send personnel and its fleet of A-10 Warthogs to support the US military operation in Afghanistan. We stood in the cold wind for several hours holding signs that read "Don't Obey Orders to Kill" and "Jesus said, 'Love your enemy.'" A security detail approached us once, but we stayed until the cold drove us back to the church.

In the morning Mary Sprunger Froese found me at the Beacon Heights Church. She was visiting from Colorado with her mother who lives near Decatur. Rich Meyer, a CPT colleague and my media support person for this trek, had been sending out email reports about my walk, one which Mary had seen to learn my whereabouts. Mary and Peter, her partner, have been radical peace activists for decades, living near Colorado Springs and witnessing regularly against the follies of nuclear war. Mary used drama, and her support of the Catholic Worker Hospitality House in Denver, among her initiatives for building peace. Mary and Peter have been part of a wide-flung network of individuals who have both inspired and encouraged me in my peacemaking ventures.

I remember when Peter and some friends freed a couple young bull buffaloes on land that was being taken over for the US Space Command Center. The buffaloes were a symbol that the land was better used as range for wild animals than to project nuclear war into space. Television news highlighted the ensuing wild and frustrating chase as military police tried vainly to capture the animals. Peter later burned his driver's license when the United States invaded Iraq in March 2003, as a protest against going to war for the oil that fuels our cars.

Mom caught up with us and the next day we traveled on to Decatur. I was averaging about twenty miles walking each day and would occasionally be joined by other walkers. I carried a small backpack with a water bottle and an extra layer of clothes most of the time in case my support vehicle got too far away from me.

This day after Christmas, Velma Shearer, and her daughter, Mary Shearer, who had been in Brethren Volunteer Service training with me thirty-three years earlier, joined me walking. Velma was in her seventies and reminded me of the Peace Pilgrim. The Peace Pilgrim walked the byways of the United States from 1953 to 1981 without money or food. She trusted that what she needed would be provided because of the goodness of people and expected that the same goodness would be her security. Everywhere she talked about the wisdom and simplicity of peace as a replacement of war.

That night a wet snow started so the next day was quite sloppy and cold. Michael Goode, CPTer from Chicago, walked with me the next two days in some pretty dire conditions. The next summer Michael would propose a walk from Boeing headquarters in Chicago to Caterpillar headquarters in Peoria, Illinois. Both companies were building equipment used to destroy the lives of Palestinian children and their parents for the Israeli occupation. That pilgrimage was a stark contrast to this one, with temperatures over one hundred degrees and no support vehicle as we carried all our gear and averaged about thirty miles per day.

Michael, Mom, Dad, and I spent the next night at the rural Ross Church of the Brethren in western Ohio. The pastor, Thom McDonald, was Native American. He was intrigued by the peacemaking work that CPT had done in conjunction with the Lakota Sioux in South Dakota and the Oneida Nation, part of the Iroquois Confederacy, in New York State.

The next day our walk took us into Lima. We stayed that night at the Salem Mennonite Church after a talk in the evening. We then drove north, off our walking track, to another Mennonite Church in Bluffton that wanted us to share there on Sunday morning. After the worship service, nearly fifty people from the congregation did a symbolic walk around the block with us, as a way to share their concern about using a war against Afghanistan to resolve differences.

ON THESE LONGER TREKS *silence is a regular companion. That silence is an opportunity to center my thoughts and hear God speaking. Silence clarifies my understanding about the issues of war, which become starkly focused as my country goes to war against a third-world country of poverty. Who are the civilian victims who pay the costs as my country wreaks technological devastation in its search for resources and revenge?*

For me, walking is an act of prayer, a way of putting feet on my prayers. I pray for those from my own country who are sent off to war. I pray for their souls, souls that are proffered up as sacrifice by those corporations, political leaders, and officers in the military machine who drive the engines of war. I pray for the people of Afghanistan, most of whom will, as civilians, be the victims of our military prowess. In wars of the last century, nearly eighty percent of the victims have been civilians. The primary victims are not the soldiers or grunts who serve as the fodder for war.

Walking combines spiritual energy and physical effort. That intersection is a spur for creativity, a necessary ingredient of peacemaking. Creativity and willingness to take risks are for me a quick-mix recipe for nonviolence, a staple for my efforts at making peace.

SEVERAL CARS RETURNED WITH me from the Bluffton Mennonite Church to the tank plant in Lima. There we formed a vigil prayer line in front of the assembly operation that was building Abrams tanks that would ship off by the thousands to the wars in west Asia.

This plant is a source of jobs for many people. But when the product of those jobs kills other people, can those jobs be justified? Is it possible for societies to organize economically in such a way that my livelihood will not lead to your death? How do groups of people remain responsible for others in their midst? When the others are far away it seems easy to ignore their reality. Peacemaking is the attempt to move closer to each other, to be cognizant of how our actions impact the other.

What if societies enticed military contractors to produce materials that build up countries and our world, instead of building for total destruction? How can economies add value to society, increase global equity? The ultimate costs of the tools of war for the home economy, if factored into the final bill, far outweigh the probable smaller profit.

Just considering the US economy, Abrams tanks are a drag on the economy compared to, say, garden hoes. The tank does nothing to add productivity. It only takes resources and production energy. Then its product, devastation, adds to the post-traumatic stress that too often takes down our soldier youths in their prime. Garden hoes require similar production lines, and their consequences, food and good health, add positively to our society. The hoe's product continues the flow of production in markets and groceries, rather than dead-ending it in destroyed buildings and infrastructure as tank production does. The produce from hoes feeds teachers who educate the next generation of students who . . .

OVER THE NEXT FEW days, temperatures plummeted below zero, but we continued to cover about twenty miles per day. New Year's Eve at a Mennonite Church with a youth party seemed a bit awkward. They didn't know quite what to do with me. But a United Methodist Church pastor took in Mom, Dad, and me the following night. We slept in the pastor's study in the church building and had a meeting with some of the church members. Then, Jeff and Jill Hardenbrook and their three children, Rachel, Sarah, and Bram, all from Dayton, joined us as we walked into Columbus.

Unknown vandals had just attacked the Islamic Center in the city. It seemed to be a racist, phobic assault targeting Muslims, similar to many other such hate crimes happening across the country. The Muslim community gathered in the large Bill McDonald Athletic Complex for Friday prayers. My parents and I decided to attend as a way to show solidarity with that hurting Muslim community. As is common, men and women were in separate sections of this large gym.

Mom remembers meeting a medical doctor from Syria. She, her husband, and two sons had been living in San Francisco when the attack on the World Trade Center happened. That west coast community treated them badly as Muslims, so they moved to the rural Midwest, hoping to find a peaceful home. The Columbus Islamic Center sustained the attack one month later.

This was the first time Mom had worshiped with Muslims, but the women welcomed her and helped her feel comfortable. Mom exudes love and care, while the Muslim women offered open arms of hospitality. For both Mom and the Muslim women, this was an important, tiny step to break down stereotypes and build bridges in a time of suspicion and hatred.

We went on from the Athletic Complex to be hosted by the Living Peace Church of the Brethren and David Jehnsen, who was nurtured under the influence of Martin Luther King Jr. and the nonviolent activism of the Civil Rights movement. We were there for the evening meal and bible study.

The next day we traveled down to the Islamic Center where there was an interfaith gathering of religious leaders to express support for the Muslim community. Folks from the Center showed us where the vandals had destroyed property and desecrated religious pieces. Media documented the attack.

Mom writes in her journal that we ate, visited, and spent that night with a United Church of Christ couple. We closed our pilgrimage with a witness against a weapons procurement plant in the morning. We three held signs reading "Jesus, Prince of Peace," "Jesus Calls us to the Cross, Not to bombs," and "4000 killed here, 4000 killed there, and How Many More?" In the afternoon we held a worship service for peace at the Capitol building in Columbus. It was quite ecumenical, with folks from different Mennonite communities, Church of the Brethren, United Methodist, and United Church of Christ communions.

We had started this pilgrimage with Gene and Doug trying to get into Afghanistan to explore putting a CPT team there. The worship service completed our pilgrimage. At this point, Gene and Doug had just arrived on a United Nations flight into Kabul, Afghanistan.

Chapter 6

Muslim Peacemaker Team, Iraq

It was during the fall of 2004 that our Muslim colleagues approached the CPT team in Baghdad with a question. "We would like to be a peacemaker team. Would you train us to be peacemakers, not Christian, but train us as a Muslim Peacemaker Team (MPT) because we are Muslim?"

It was a very logical question. They had been one of the groups CPT had connected with regularly for direction in our peace efforts while in Iraq. On their own initiative they had been involved in some dramatic peace building efforts. Najaf had been under attack by the US military because Muqtada al Sadr, a very anti-US Iraqi nationalist Shia cleric, was holed up with his militia in the religious center of that city. This pre-MPT group had helped organize a nonviolent march into that city. The march broke the tensions in such a way that both fighting groups could stand down from the violence and still save face. It also protected the civilian population that would have been decimated by the US onslaught and ensuing street battles.

Was our CPT training cross cultural and interreligious? Yes, we had already had many applicants from other cultures that had been through CPT training. That was not an issue. We were overtly Christian but that wouldn't seem to prevent us from training Muslims to be peacemakers.

In CPT's early years we had been working in communities where other faiths were predominant. In Israel, this meant we had times we worked closely with rabbis and other Jews. In Gaza and the West Bank, many of the folks with whom we worked as colleagues were Muslim. In Chiapas,

Mexico, the Las Abejas groups were mostly Christian, but there were also those who held with traditional Mayan religion and we worked as well with them. However, in none of these cases had there been an agreement to a request to train them as peacemakers!

This call in Iraq was complicated by the security situation. In the fall of 2004, the resistance and anger against the US military occupation was exploding. Radical Wahabi fighters from Saudi Arabia had gained influence in the so-called "death triangle" south of Baghdad. Driving through that region to Kerbala and Najaf for the training meant we could be stopped at a Wahabi checkpoint.

Checkpoints are a way of life in military zones. We could face trouble at either US or Iraqi checkpoints. They might choose to turn us back to Baghdad. But stories from the Wahabi checkpoints were that anyone who was Shia or Christian risked losing their head by way of a sword. There was no jury or judge. Those staffing that traffic stop made their own autonomous call and executed the judgment on the spot.

Our drivers would be Shia and it would probably be assumed rather quickly and correctly that we passengers were Christian. I doubt if any of our team in Baghdad were any more willing than others to risk their necks, but some of us felt this training request was at an opportune moment.

We first traveled south to check out the idea more thoroughly and test the route. Doug Pritchard, co-director of CPT, was with us at that time and joined the trip. We needed a good trusted translator, a committed group of trainees, an open time frame for busy people, a workable space for the training activities, and support arrangements like food and lodging. Those details fell into place and CPT decided this training would be a good plan.

Peggy Gish, Maxine Nash, Alan Slater, and I headed south for the training in early January 2005. We traveled in two vehicles and carried phones in case we needed to communicate. The women wore shawls and were well covered; we men wrapped in kafiyas which did something to disguise our foreignness. There were edgy parts of the trip but the checkpoints were not Wahabi.

One key part of CPT training is strengthening the spiritual undergirding that will carry us through the impossible situations that will confront us in our journey of peacebuilding. As a Christian, I look to the spiritual undergirding of prayer, fasting, silence, a community of support, walking, devotions, and journaling. We didn't know where our Shia sisters and brothers would point for their spiritual undergirding. But prayer, fasting, worship, and support community were common themes for them too.

This period in Iraq was a time of change, as every period turned out to be. The US assault on Fallujah had just taken place in November and

December. At the size of Fort Wayne, Indiana, the city of Fallujah was destroyed to save it. Seventy percent of the homes were demolished or so badly damaged as to be unlivable.

January was also only ten months away from the moment four CPTers became hostages for one hundred eighteen days. They were held by a radical Muslim group and released only after the killing of CPTer Tom Fox following his apparent release.

CPT had just completed an in-depth documentation of over seventy cases of detention of Iraqis by the US and allied Iraqi forces. We carried this report to the highest-ranking US political and military leaders in Iraq with the warning of anger building against the US occupation. The report was a lead up to Seymour Hersh's later revelations of torture of Iraqi detainees by US security and military forces in Abu Ghraib Prison and other US military detention centers across the country.

January 2005 was just over one month before the bombing of the Shia shrine in Samara. This destruction was to open a huge chasm between the Sunni and Shia Muslim sects of Iraq. Manufactured by the US, according to some of our sources, this turned the Iraqi anger against the US into a national sectarian volcano instead. This explosion of anger and frustration came to dominate the political events across Iraq in the ensuing months.

For now, the CPT team was split between Baghdad and Kerbala. The four in Kerbala were immersed in the training of a Muslim Peacemaker Team! We did role plays to see how trainees would respond in volatile situations and then debriefed the exercises. What did trainees do well? What could trainees have done differently? What creative intervention might have turned the violence from a disaster to a transformation?

What are the instruments of nonviolence we carry in our imaginary peacemaking kits? What nonviolent actions have we already done? Which ones are individual and which require a group? What does a campaign of nonviolence look like? What tools do we need to develop to be better prepared for what is down the road in front of us? What are the weaknesses in the methods we already have that need shoring up?

We examined the risks of nonviolent peacemaking. How will we respond as authorities or opposition groups crack down on our actions? How do we deal with harassment, torture or prison? How do we maintain nonviolence in the face of extreme violence against us? Have we written our wills?

We carried out training in media work and documentation of events through stories and photography. Often the media version is the only one that will make it into the public arena. How can we assure that it is done well? Are there techniques to guarantee that the various perspectives get into the story? A timely photo can tell the entire story.

I recall the photo that made the front page of the Toronto Star during the CPT support of the Esgenoopetitj First Nation campaign in New Brunswick, Canada. A Royal Canadian Mounted Police (RCMP) crew in a powerful speedboat was ramming through/over a tiny First Nation craft out picking up lobster traps. The issues came alive. The attempt by white fisherman, supported by the RCMP and the Bureau of Fisheries and Oceans, to keep the aboriginal crews from setting traps, just ruled as legal by the Canadian Supreme Court, was now out in the open.

In Kerbala, one of the sisters, Amira, used a broken heart, a pink paper in the shape of a heart torn in pieces, to illustrate her point that trauma strikes each one of us in this kind of setting. Most everyone in the training group shared a very personal and painful story. How will we deal with trauma? If we can't find ways to heal from it, we will be severely handicapped in our peacemaking.

At the finish of the successful training we queried what steps were next, what will you as a Muslim Peacemaker Team do now? They said they wanted to take peacemaker trainings across Iraq. They already knew of groups hungering for this expertise. They wanted to go to Darfur, Sudan, to take their peacemaking skills to that tragic place. And they wanted to take their new skills to the United States; it needed peacemaking! "But," we asked, "What will you do first?'

"Let's go to Fallujah and start to rebuild that city, just destroyed by the US," suggested one new MPTer.

"That can never work," responded another. "The city, mostly Sunni, now has an entirely Shia police force, set in place by the US. It is a volatile place. The people would never stand for our mostly Shia presence. We would be attacked or killed."

"But our training never said that peacemaking would not be dangerous," retorted one of the leaders who had helped pull this group together initially.

So it happened. One of them telephoned a Sunni cleric in Fallujah. That religious leader was a bit incredulous but suggested it would be good to start on cleanup so that rebuilding could then proceed. MPT arrived in Fallujah, dressed in orange vests, and worked through the day with others from that destroyed city. At the end of the day the cleric was ecstatic!

"This kind of action is great. We should put together a team of Shia and Sunni and go to Kirkuk in the Kurdish north and clean up that community. Then we should form a team of Kurds, Sunnis and Shias and travel all across this country to rebuild."

Truly, this would have transformed and pulled Iraq together! With the occupation tearing Iraq into pieces, and the bombing of the Samarra shrine on the heels of this training visit, this joint effort across sectarian lines would have been the mending action for a new Iraq. This dream team did not happen. But other things did happen.

Some years later MPT held another training in Najaf. This seemed to gather more professional, medical, and scientific people. It happened solely from the initiative and energy of the first MPT unit. CPT was already in the north of Iraq by then. This new group carried out extensive studies on the impact of US depleted uranium weapons on the region around Najaf in the south of the country.

As I write this, I realize the opportunity to share with the MPT group in Iraq the information in Chapter 20 on the DU Campaign here in the United States!

The MPT group also visited twice with CPT and Kurdish groups in Sulaymaniyah in the north. I was there the first time. I remember meeting a physicist who had been working on early US-assisted nuclear developments under former President Saddam Hussein. The physicist had fled oppression in his home country in the late nineties. He came back only after the start of the war, when he saw an opportunity to shape what Iraq would become, at risk to himself.

This MPT group has been nurturing sister city relationships with cities in the US. Sami Rasouli was the translator during the first training CPT carried out. He had lived in the US for twelve years and had a fine restaurant in Minneapolis. He became the point person for the sister city efforts and for MPT as an entity.

When our Rutbah group (see chapter 11) went back into Iraq in 2010, Sami was the "fixer" and "minder" for our trip. The trip would not have taken place without the extreme efforts that Sami put into it. He spoke English very well and understood Americans as well as anyone can from another culture. His sons still live in the US, though Sami, his wife, and more recently born children live in Najaf where many of his extended family live. When the US invasion was approaching in 2003, Sami saw what was about to take place. He made the decision that German theologian and eventual martyr Dietrich Bonhoeffer made as WWII was approaching. He returned to his home to see what he could do to stop the war.

The training of the Muslim Peacemaker Team by CPT was one of the most important activities we did in Iraq. Local people can do much more than outsiders who parachute into a crisis. The local language is their native tongue. Their culture has ways of operating and changing that only they are privy to. Locals already know some of the change tools that are indigenous to the region. They have ready allies where outsiders have to build those alliances. May Allah, Almighty God, help MPT go far!

Chapter 7

Fear and I in Nigeria

Roy Winter, director of Brethren Disaster Ministries (BDM) asked me to go to Nigeria in the late fall of 2014. I would serve for three months as a link between BDM and the newly formed Crisis Management Team of Ekklesiyar Yan'uwa a Nigeria (EYN, the Church of the Brethren in Nigeria). He wanted someone who wouldn't freak out at the sound of an explosion down the street. I guess my experiences in CPT gave me some credibility.

Fear of Boko Haram has a major impact on the people of EYN today. Fear has driven most of the members of EYN to move from their homes. That fear determines where I am allowed to travel in 2015 as one who works with EYN. That same fear shaped the impressions that members of the Church of the Brethren in the US have of Nigeria.

Fear is the primary tool of violence. Fear is used to immobilize an enemy. Fear can terrorize and incapacitate an enemy. Fear prevents an enemy from considering ways to overcome its power. Fear is used by Boko Haram. Fear is used by Al Qaeda; the attack on the World Trade Center was an act to stimulate fear. Fear is used by the Islamic State. Of course, the Islamic State refined its tactics in the prisons and torture chambers of the United States, in the US-controlled Abu Ghraib Prison in Iraq. Fear was also used there.

Boko Haram is a new manifestation of fear. It is mostly invisible because few people from the outside have spent time with this group. Those who have experienced the violence of Boko Haram are often immobilized by the shock of the acts carried out by them. *How is a group like ours to initiate contact with Boko Haram? What if burial teams of Christians and Muslims went into the areas conceded to Boko Haram and offered to bury bodies? Those teams might take back conceded space in their willingness to face down fear.*

Night and invisibility assist the growth of terror. Boko Haram has learned its lessons well. Surely torture and fear have a long bloody history. The torture chambers of the Inquisition, the hell holes of the Nazi Holocaust, the cells of Guantanamo Prison, and the hidden rendition sites of the United States all are training schools for terror and terrorist groups. Their invisibility allows public imagination to blow things out of proportion, overestimating their power. Then glimpses of them can be used to increase fear, terror, and control.

The training manual of the School of the Americas (Fort Benning, Georgia) refined the tools of fear. Those tools of fear became the implements to "re-form" civil society to fit the needs of Empire. So religious leaders, political activists, union leaders, human rights workers, and ordinary farmers became targets of pressure, torture, and death. Similar fear and domination training exists within the Israeli military and police, with whom US police often train. The experiences of Israeli security forces, and the implements used to destroy Palestinian society, are marketed around the world for dominant political societies to control or eliminate their opposition.

Learning to deal with fear is an important requirement for nonviolence practitioners, especially followers of the Prince of Peace. The Bible is full of passages that debunk fear. There are the angel's words to Zachariah in the temple (Luke 1:11—13); to Mary when she was told she would carry the Messiah (Luke 1:28—30); to the shepherds caring for their flocks in the dark of night (Luke 2:8—11); and Jesus' words to his disciples hidden behind locked doors (Luke 24:36—39). These are all words to alleviate fear and build courage for the road ahead.

I compare the learning process to Arlene's steps in preparing to cook for large numbers of people. She is a good cook, but she didn't start out cooking for a crowd of three hundred. I don't start out facing Boko Haram in the village streets of Gwoza, their center of operation in eastern Nigeria. But I do want to reach the place where I would be willing to go there.

What if a team went to take gifts to the leaders of Boko Haram? Going with gifts of one thousand moringa tree starts (miracle healing tree of Nigeria), a peace choir from the women's fellowship (ZME) of EYN, a plethora of nonviolent tools to replace the dysfunctional violent tools they use, and a trauma healing team of Muslims and Christians? Acting with this spirit counteracts fear.

JUST NOW (FEBRUARY 2020), *a news report crosses my screen. Boko Haram insurgents have attacked Garkida, the site where Church of the Brethren missionaries in Nigeria first gathered for worship under a tamarind tree in 1923. The attack targeted the police station, a health clinic, and three churches. The assault from numerous pickups and motorcycles took several hours. No police or military interrupted the raid.*

I recall preparing an initiative at a Church of the Brethren Annual Conference in Columbus, Ohio, in 2014. It was a risky offer by ten of us to be exchanged to Boko Haram for the release of the nearly 300 young women students kidnapped by them from Chibok two months earlier. Both the delegates at our Annual Conference in Ohio and, later, leaders of EYN in Nigeria objected to the danger and blocked the action. Would we still be facing aggressions from Boko Haram if we had boldly and creatively engaged their leaders and foot soldiers at that early stage? Sometimes being larger than our fears may lead to initiatives that are worth the risks.

WHEN ARLENE PREPARES RAISED donuts for three hundred people she works in a favorable context: 1) She has cooked donuts often; 2) she has helpers; 3) she has favorite recipes which she has tested; 4) she has utensils that expedite the process; 5) she has spaces to let the dough rise, cook in hot fat, cool and hang from dripping racks after icing; and 6) she has tables to feed hungry people.

When I visit a war zone, I try to build a favorable intervention context by reading all I can find about the place. I also pray while working in the garden. I dream scenarios of possible situations and my responses. And I go by invitation, so I know that there are others to walk with me—teammates with whom I will work.

I have practiced fear management in other places while working with Christian Peacemaker Teams. When suicide bombers came to our house in Baghdad, or when armed robbers raided our compound in the Democratic Republic of the Congo, we spent hours debriefing the experiences. Deconstructing the experiences helps me to understand the pieces of fear and also how to deal with the trauma.

Yes, trauma does affect most of us in these and other types of situations. Trauma healing works to frame the experience in ways other than terror. Trauma is our body's safety fuse that blows when fear is about to overwhelm our body's capacity to cope. But then trauma comes back to haunt us, because the normal emotional circuits have been broken. They need to be rebuilt through long patient work.

Forgiveness is an action that can change the dynamics and understanding of an event. Also, if I can understand the violence and fear in a way that allows me to envision a positive future, I regain control of my responses in both energizing and life-giving ways. So dealing with fear both before and after it happens, and doing it many times, allows me to understand the construction and deconstruction of fear. Maybe this somewhat parallels the ease with which Arlene can undertake a cooking assignment for a large group of people.

Realizing that fear impacts any nonviolent actions that I may participate in helps me to recognize my reactions to fear and move to minimize its effect, so that I can be the one who takes the initiative rather than being immobilized by the fear that an "enemy" throws down at me.

What if we held a fifty-thousand-person march from central Nigeria toward the northeast where Boko Haram is ensconced? It would attract heavy media coverage. Muslims and Christians would make up the marchers since both are about equally impacted by Boko Haram's violence. Invite the Catholic archbishop, the Muslim Emir of Kano, and Pope Francis to participate. Take the choir of ZME, the Muslim youth who protected the churches of Christians during Christmas celebrations, and the Christian youth who protected the mosques during Muslim holy days. The message would be that together we desire a different and better future than what Boko Haram is creating. Clearly, a caliphate with no people, with wells containing dead bodies, destroyed homes and schools, burned medical clinics, and destroyed harvests does not lead to a workable future. So, invite Boko Haram to help shape the future in ways that all benefit.

I CARRY METHODS THAT counteract fear too. The New Testament is full of tools that retake the initiative for peace. Paul invites us to overcome evil with good (Romans 12:21); and to feed our enemies if they are hungry and give them something to drink if they are thirsty (Romans 12:20). Jesus says to love our enemies by praying for those who persecute us (Matthew 5:44); and to love our enemies by doing good to those who hate us ((Luke 6:27—28). He said that the peacemakers are blessed (Matthew 5:9)! These are the implements and processes that plowshare violence and injustice.

I have experienced that when I get to the place where my concern is for the wholeness of the other, or the wholeness of humanity, I can risk love. At that point, concern for myself becomes minimal. I am in the place where a gift of a moringa tree, or food or any sort of goodness, is bigger than either of us, with the power to change us both for the better. I can take the risk. In that risk, "enemy" disappears.

Sure, we could encourage Nigeria to do what the United States military did in Iraq and Afghanistan, Somalia and Libya, Syria and Yemen. But I don't wish that on Nigeria. I think we have much more effective skills at our disposal. The suggestions I have peppered through this chapter may or may not be the ones for Nigeria to choose, but perhaps they can stimulate even better and more creative ideas for Nigerian peacemakers to use.

Ananias in Acts 9:10—19 is resistant to the prodding of Jesus because of his fear, but finally agrees to lay hands on Saul, a Boko Haram-style leader persecuting the early church. In that laying on of hands Saul regains his sight and receives the Holy Spirit. He is transformed, as is Ananias. Ananias moves from resisting any contact with his enemy because of fear, to laying his hands on the enemy for healing. Saul moves from ravaging the church (Acts 8:3) to being an advocate of that same Way (Acts 9:18—22). This Saul, also known as Paul, goes on to write about half of our New Testament.

So where are the Ananiases in Nigeria who, in spite of their fear, will lay hands on the Sauls of Boko Haram? One needs to be close to them to do that, close enough to share some of Arlene's donuts with Boko Haram.

FEAR IS A GENUINE human emotion. We should not ignore or belittle it. We should not fall prey to the easy trap of using it against others. In parenting, teaching, campaigning, police work, conflict or any other situation, we need to be more creative. If we use fear, we make ourselves smaller. We cut off the potential of the person with whom we are interacting to also use their creativity, in order to help us resolve the issue we together are facing. If your actions push me into my fear mode, I easily accept the lone option you place before me, and you also stop being stimulated to think bigger. In war, we end up with cycles of violence against each other because fear has short circuited our mutual creativity.

In trauma healing, telling my story over and over provides a way out of fear's short circuit. In the telling, I can remember the ways I was strong in the midst of the traumatic event. I can begin to see ways others were there carrying me. In that eye-opening process, I am allowed to see a potentially different future from the fear-trauma cycle I have been stuck in. In that development of a positive future, I have begun healing from the trauma. I have regained my life.

The speaking tours I went on after my project in Gaza, and my five stints in Iraq, were lifesavers for me. Telling the same stories over and over provided the space to begin the healing process in my life. This is important for all those dealing with PTSD (post-traumatic stress disorder) from military experiences—to be granted a space to tell their stories to others who will hear those events gracefully.

Chapter 8

In Boko Haram's Wake

I was in Nigeria during 2015 when Ekklesiyar Yan'uwa a Nigeria, EYN, was in the midst of the catastrophe that was Boko Haram. Displaced families were still scrambling for a safe place to land. Emergency food distributions were carrying people from day to day. The EYN leadership was still shaping an entirely new Crisis Management Team that was itself mired in the overwhelming trauma.

In January 2017, I was in Nigeria again. I was a cog in the nine-member team from the Church of the Brethren (COB) for the EYN/COB Workcamp under the supervision of BEST (Brethren Evangelism Support Trust). BEST is comprised of Nigerian business and church leaders. Our COB team visited five of the communities that I had spent time in during my previous visit. Things had changed!

The devastation imploding in the wake of Boko Haram during 2015 was palpable. The violence targeted churches and mosques with bombings and burnings. Schools and clinics were in the center of the bullseye. Homes and businesses were leveled. Human beings, both Muslims and Christians, became the casualties of kidnappings and brutal killings. Wells served as the repository for dead bodies. Bridges were no longer passages over rivers, as their bombed wreckage blocked easy transit. The powers of death can easily wreak destruction over a wide landscape. The northeast of Nigeria lay in shambles.

In 2017, our work camp had the task of helping build a church for displaced families who had fled from Chibok. Readers may remember that this is the community where Boko Haram had kidnapped nearly three hundred young women from their school in April of 2014. Our work was just one building in a denomination that needed a thousand churches built or rebuilt! It was fairly insignificant in the larger scale of things, but clearly symbolic of something more dramatic happening.

As I write, we are just three weeks from the beginning of Lent. Lent is a season that exposes the spiritual struggle between the powers of death and the powers of life. In Jesus, the powers of death do their worst, but life and the spirit of love in the Creator's resurrection drama swallow death up in victory (I Corinthians 15: 54). Death no longer has dominion. Lent is taking place in Nigeria.

At the EYN guest house where we stayed in Abuja, a new primary school is growing on the first and third floors for about seventy young students. At the Masaka Community, which was bush land when I visited two years ago, there are seventy homes occupied, a solar powered water well, and a four-room school for the two hundred children now living there. In the Gurku interfaith community, where seventy mud brick homes were just being completed when I last visited, there is now a Montessori school, a new church building completed, and a mosque on the drawing board to be constructed in a joint community project. Yes, here too is a model for Muslims and Christians to live together, caring for each other's widows, and opening their well (with solar panels providing the energy to pump the water) to the nomadic Muslim Fulani herders as they pass through this region with their flocks. In Chinka, where two years ago the Kulp Bible College had landed when their campus in the northeast came under attack, there is now an emergent secondary school with the dream of a university on those eighty hectares (about two hundred acres) of land. This is the site of a scheduled April EYN/COB Workcamp to build a new dormitory on the foundation nearly hidden in the brush and piles of earth.

Malnutrition and starvation are rampant now in Nigeria. Part of the response to this crisis is to provide seeds and farm implements to the EYN families and Muslim neighbors who are returning to their lands. Yes, the northeast breadbasket of Nigeria was leveled but the soil and the skills are still rich and resilient. The rainy season is but one month away. Can people survive until the crops come in? Maybe seventy percent of the EYN displaced have returned home. What kind of hope undergirds this return?

In the Masaka local EYN church north of Abuja, Arlene and I participated in worship on our second Sunday. The throb of the drums echoed the beat of human hearts and the deeper beat of the earth in its sustainable echo of the love of the Creator. The *six* choirs filled that space with a spirit that is anything but in the doldrums of despair. How can it be that a body that has experienced such horrors can reflect a joy that not only reaches above the despair, but overwhelms the negative spiritual power of all that death and destruction?

Well, the church in the New Testament resonates with that kind of joy. EYN is a reflection of that same spirit. It is genuine gospel exuberance, the content which is the power of mission. So I bring back a report of that spirit in EYN. They have become the missionaries to the church that first sent missionaries to Nigeria soon one hundred years ago. Are we open to that kind of gospel where the power of love is lived as stronger than the power of hate, exclusion, and death? Time will tell the further story, both there and here.

Chapter 9

Baghdad, Living in the Bullseye

By January 2003, about *fifty of us from Christian Peacemaker Teams and Voices in the Wilderness had united to form the Iraq Peace Team. For the three months we had already been in Iraq, we had assumed a US invasion aimed at Baghdad was imminent. I sent this poem as an open letter to our daughter Miriam in January as an expression of the powerful feelings surging over my soul.*

Dear daughter of my blood, compassionate Sister of the human race,
We have raced the wind, side by side on our bikes, dragging the breath of life into our lungs
As we hit the marsh flats on the straightaway headed for Joyfield Farm.

I write from the center of the universe, the beginning of creation,
Where the Tigris and Euphrates flow together at the Garden of Eden, several hundred miles south of Baghdad.
My housing rises from the earth between the two rivers, the Fertile Crescent, the birthplace of civilization.
This is the land of Ur, the place from which Sarah and Abraham set out on a journey that led to the action of faith (Genesis 11:31).

I write from the lands nurtured by the wells of the Spirit,

The sea deeps from which Jonah was spit out toward Nineveh
(Jonah 2:10—3:3),
The prayer deeps that carried Daniel, Shadrach, and company
(Daniel 3).

I write from the center of hell, the seething, swirling maelstrom
that threatens to capsize our souls.
I've stood in the pit from which Daniel was pulled away from
the closed jaws of the lions (Daniel 6, esp. verse 22).
I've parked my body where the United States dumped 500 tons
of depleted uranium (DU),
Sowing death on the earth for 4.5 billion years.

You were with me in the DU-ridden downwind trade winds of
Vieques.
We were the largest Christian Peacemaker Teams delegation on
the ground ever.
And you, yes, you Sister, are one of the reasons I'm in CPT.
"Daddy, maybe we should make it possible for you to go to Gaza.
There sons and fathers leave home and never return, you are
only going for three months."

I write from today's Auschwitzian ovens. These gases are radioactive and economic.
Five thousand children a month die from leukemia, diarrhea,
and water-borne diseases.
The war brought the cancers and the sanctions stopped the repair of water treatment plants.

I write from the center of death where the rivers of life have
become the rivers of hell.
Friday I was deeply moved at the Chaldean Christian school
Peggy and I visited.
The exuberant smiles and handshakes, children ages 3–21, burst
my carefully constructed dam.

I built the dam after Gaza.
"As you cross the border into Gaza you cross the border into
hell," said Rabbi Jeremy.
It was brutal. I cried deeper in my soul than I've ever cried
before.
One can't live. Too much anger. Too much pain. One must dam
the tears.

I strengthened the dam in the memorial building of Acteal, 45 massacred by paramilitaries.
And again on La Framboise Island with the Lakota warriors protecting their land and people, nonviolently.
I shored it up in Rio Nuevo Ité as the bananas were planted and the chickens hatched
While the band of 500 military and paramilitary still roamed the campo.
I built the dam as high as Aswan in New Brunswick with Miiga-mahan and Geesatanamuk.

Yesterday the high dam was breached by an eroding rivulet that threatens a flood.
We've worked the floods of Riley and Fort Wayne,
The storms of Mount Olive and Mobile, the furies of Culebra and Caimito.

Here the Flood once washed clean (Genesis 6—9), but now the flood, or as Baldwin writes, "The Fire Next Time," threatens to engulf us.
The Gulf War burned deep
Etched on our souls, it trained the Oklahoma City bomber as he plowed under the surrendering Iraqi soldiers for two days after the cease fire on the Road of Death.
"It was a turkey shoot," proclaimed the US soldiers as they brought the war home.

It was reborn in their babies—without eyes, organs outside their bodies, without brains—
And in the D.C. sniper who learned his lessons well.

I write from the land of empires, built and collapsed—Babylon, Assyria, Alexander, and Babel.
Here God looked down on the tower (Genesis 11:3—5).
Here are the ruins of empire, the grave of Alexander.

Dear Miriam, sister of Moses and Aaron, the one who danced as the winds held back the floods,
The one who walked through on dry land, who watched as the waters terminated empire (Genesis 15:20—21).

Dear Miriam, Mary, mother of Jesus, there as the birth waters broke, the healing river.

The one who watched, nurtured, pondered, wept as the cross-
winds of salvation bucked empire and lifted humanity (Luke
2:6—19 and John 19:25).

Well, Sister, where is the saving flood?
Where today the healing waters of Pentecost (Acts 2:1—4, 41)?
As Empire emerges from the wellspring of Hell,
Is there a Body willing to be nailed to the cross with its Jesus, in
resistance to this powerful Legion?
Does the resurrection live in the scattered "least of these?"

Miriam, you who held the abandoned ones in your arms at the
Catholic Worker houses in San Antonio,
Where are the arms to hold these 23 million, abandoned for 12
years to the manipulated intrigues of oil, money, and power?

Here in Iraq are the wells that fuel the engines of empire.
Where are the wells that undergird us enough to battle for Life
in the depths of horror we must enter today?

Compassionate Sister, what is the dance that will celebrate the
waters held back here?
Is He still Lord of the dance?

Love, Dad

Chapter 10

Transparency and Accountability

IN 2010, I WROTE and attempted to send a letter to Bradley, now Chelsea, Manning. Manning was accused in the press of leaking a massive trove of US government files to WikiLeaks. My letter was written and sent but was not delivered, because Manning was held in solitary confinement under very strict mailing and visitation privileges.

When I wrote my letter, there had not even been charges filed against Manning. Psychiatrists testified that confinement conditions at the Marine Corps Brig in Quantico, Virginia, were those under which most normal persons would be severely psychologically damaged or destroyed. Officers kept Manning under those conditions despite requests from the military psychiatrist that the conditions be improved for her mental health.

It appears that the US government may bring charges of treason against Manning. At the same time there may be an attempt to encourage her to reveal information against Julian Assange in exchange for a lighter sentence. Julian Assange is the visible face of the WikiLeaks movement. There have been US political and media figures who have said Assange should be assassinated or targeted by drones. At this writing, he was moved from his place of asylum granted by Ecuador, at their embassy in London, to solitary confinement prior to an extradition trial.

Assange and the WikiLeaks movement have stated their goal to make available to the public political information that is usually hidden. So diplomatic cables, economic information about hidden bank accounts, human rights violations such as those done under the Suharto dictatorship in Indonesia, and military actions by various countries around the world are being brought to light.

It is a different tool from that which activists usually employ. Well, it is similar to the release of the Pentagon Papers in 1971 by Daniel Ellsburg during the Vietnam War, but on a scale that makes that action look like a high school news release. The Wikileaks release has major popular support from around the world, except from those who have been embarrassed or exposed by the revelations.

THIS ISSUE RAISES IMPORTANT *questions. What actions are valid use of nonviolent tools? These leaks of government papers are nonviolent actions. How do we judge it in terms of effectiveness, morality, rightness? Are the Plowshares actions which did symbolic physical damage to US nuclear weapons and their launch facilities properly included in nonviolence? Is the release of "classified" information that may uncover the identity of a spy, among other state secrets, to be considered outside the boundary of nonviolence? Or inside? Is the placing of provocateurs into a circle of nonviolent activists by government security groups a nonviolent action?*

How do nonviolent groups work with the understanding that there is a high likelihood there are attempts to compromise their efforts by such undercover agitators? In the field with CPT, I was often aware that it would be easy for such groups to derail our peacemaking actions. A nonviolent activist team must be squeaky clean. We must try our best to not provide reasons to discredit the cause. Often in other countries that could simply be the breach of cultural sensitivities that would turn the public against us.

More seriously, drug, alcohol, or sexual compromises can allow an undercover agent to weaken or divert the peacemaking struggle through enticements and loss of mental acuity. How do we, as often young, idealistic activists, maintain our spirit of risky emotional engagement without compromising the peace building goals? One of the strengths of CPT teams has been the rich mix of race, age, gender, culture, sexual orientation, and skills that each team member has brought to the struggle with those unique individual advantages.

I remember, at the end of a seven hundred hour fast in the West Bank, against the planned seven hundred Israeli demolitions of Palestinian homes, we were beginning to rebuild a house that had been demolished a year earlier. That demolition was against the order of the Israeli Prime Minister who had ordered it to stop. But the demolition went ahead when Israeli settlers living on the land illegally urged the soldiers to complete the task. We were CPTers, other internationals including World Vision, a Jewish rabbi, and Palestinian youths. After declaring a closed military zone and threatening arrest of any who remained, Israeli police started to arrest us. They arrested the two Palestinian youths, then me, then the Jewish rabbi, but they would not touch CPTer Anne Montgomery. Anne was then a seventy-one-year-old Catholic sister who continued clearing concrete chunks from the top of the pile of rubble that used to be a home. The younger police still had respect for older women. This age and gender diversity added strength to the composition of our CPT team.

Anne was the daughter of a WWII admiral who was in the Pacific theater. I guess his "pacific" nature passed on in his genes. Anne was frequently among the mostly Catholic Plowshares activists in their actions against nuclear war. She told me about canoeing and swimming out to a nuclear submarine off Groton, Connecticut, in the cold waters of the Atlantic at age fifty-five with a small sledgehammer in one hand. After hours in the chilly waters she beat on that huge war machine as a symbolic action to plowshare it (Isaiah 2:4) into something that would be beneficial for humankind.

WikiLeaks explains how the release of tightly held knowledge makes available to citizens information that allows educated decisions about policies. It levels the playing field between government leaders and citizens. It makes it easier to hold leaders accountable to their citizens for their actions.

Government leaders and others who feel negatively impacted by the WikiLeaks-type revelations have responded in anger at the releases. They claim these releases will destroy trust in international relations. They say the releases will make it more difficult to build negotiated, rather than military, responses to crises. The United States Justice Department would like to extradite Assange so he can be charged in court.

It is interesting to note that, at a time when US Homeland Security measures are opening up more personal emails, phone calls, and Twitter/Facebook communications to government scrutiny, the opening of government communication to public scrutiny is seen as a criminal offense or a treasonous action. Are there limits to these kinds of nonviolent actions (release of government documents or plowshare acts)? Who should set limits if there are any?

Chapter 11

Good Samaritan from Iraq

IN LATE OCTOBER 2002, I traveled to Iraq with Kathy Kelly, Thorne Anderson, and Jeremy Scahill. We were part of a joint effort between Voices in the Wilderness and Christian Peacemaker Teams to stop the war. Over the next five months, we traveled all over Iraq with multiple delegations from around the world, to show the disasters of the First Gulf War and the ensuing thirteen years of sanctions. Our hope was to display the humanness of the Iraqis who would be the victims of any upcoming war. We were educators, farmers, health professionals, legislators, writers, artists, musicians, activists, students, social workers, businesspeople, retired military, professors, and other retirees. The range of ages for this Iraq Peace Team was from early twenties to ninety-six.

What would it take to stop a war? If grandmothers and grandfathers were on the ground before the bombers flew, would that stop the war? Imagine a fighter pilot ready to loose his missiles on a target below. "Wait a minute! Grandma is down there. No way!"

I met a man in Georgia who had been a US fighter pilot while President Reagan was in office. He was regularly in the squadron of fighter jets flying low over Libya to provoke an attack, so the bombers high overhead could justify dropping their loads targeting Colonel Muammar Qaddafi below. At one point the US fighter pilot came to his senses: "What am I doing? This action is trying to start a war and I'll be the first casualty! I am out of here." He turned back and left the Air Force. So, it does happen.

What if former President Jimmy Carter or Jesse Jackson had gone to Iraq to stop the war? Certainly, President Bush, Donald Rumsfeld, and Dick Cheney would not have initiated a conflict then!

OR WHAT IF POPE John Paul II had been in Iraq? In fact, as the invasion was starting, Jim Douglass had stopped at the Vatican to talk with cardinals about having the Pope join him as Jim went into Iraq on the last CPT delegation. The Pope was not well then, so it did not take place. But what if it had?

Jim had made that request before in Sarajevo, when the city was being bombarded regularly from the surrounding hills. What if he had been able to get prominent Catholic, Muslim, and Orthodox leaders to stand together in that city and call for a halt to that violence?

Dick Cheney's daughter had called from Amman in February asking to join us peacemakers in Baghdad, Iraq. What if she had been able to get in before her dad flew on an overnight jet to Amman to talk her out of that logical action? Would the bombing have started if she was there? What would it take to stop a war? Could we stop a war?

We didn't, and it became clear that the US invasion was going to happen. A teammate from Voices, a pastor/lawyer from Perth, Australia, estimated we had about a forty percent chance of coming out of the US invasion alive. Therefore, we really encouraged anyone who had any question about staying to return home. Would that each Iraqi had been granted the same opportunity to leave!

We prepared for the invasion by learning emergency operation procedures from one of our physician colleagues in case we were unable to access a hospital. We stashed water and dates for survival since markets might fail and water might shut down. We split into two groups and two hotels, so one group might survive. We boarded up the windows of the small hotel in which we lived.

It was 2:30 a.m. on March 20 when we got the call from CNN in Basrah: "The missiles have been fired and the bombers are on the way. You have three hours." We gathered with lit candles on the first floor as a team. We prayed, read some scripture, sang a song, and shared some of the emotions that were flooding over us.

It was minutes or seconds after 5:35 a.m. when the bowels of the earth seemed to open up and hell poured out. One of Saddam Hussein's palaces was just across the Tigris River from our hotel. The missiles screamed through the air. The heavy thud of bombs dropping and the whine of futile anti-aircraft weapons fire filled the airspace over a city of three million human beings created in God's image.

I had just written in my small notebook: "Rooster crowed three times. President Bush is the betrayer of the world." At 5:35, my notes read, "Felt an explosion, heard a muffled sound, a plane in the air, and the air raid siren."

After two hours of madness, there was silence. We caught a taxi to carry our tent and supplies to the Al Wathba Water Treatment Plant. During and after the First Gulf War, the allied coalition had targeted water facilities. According to the United Nations, this led to the death of 500,000 children because of impure water over the next decade. Our tent was to be a symbol of the vulnerability of civilians. Canvas won't even stop a rifle bullet, let alone a missile or a bomb.

Over the next ten days, we seemed to be the news source of the world. Few journalists had stayed. We took calls from Europe, Africa, South America, Asia, and from our home cities across North America. Along with our presence at the plant, our CPT and Voices colleagues were visiting hospitals and sites where "smart bombs" had killed civilians as they targeted hospital grounds, markets, and residential neighborhoods.

At night I would stand out by the pools of water and listen to the sounds of war: missiles whooshing through the air over my head; the deep rumble of bombers on their regular runs; the scream of fighter jets cutting through the night sky; and the responding chatter of anti-aircraft fire. I could hear the splash of spent bullets into the water behind me. All fifty of us lived through the first ten days of "Shock and Awe."

Ten days into the assault, a missile took out the communication center close to our hotel. For the first time, we had no phone service to call a taxi. So we walked to our regular Iraq Peace Team meeting. On the way we passed the intersection from which we could look back to the targeted communication building.

We asked a police officer on the circle if we could go see it. "Welcome," he said, but others in the city were not so eager to offer welcome. Iraqi Mukabarat, the secret police, rounded us up, held us at a police station, and then ordered us out of the country immediately. By then it was late afternoon. It would have meant traveling through the night to cross three hundred miles of the western desert where the fighting was still hot.

I expect it was Kathy Kelly who negotiated instead an early morning departure for the eight of us rounded up, two Japanese journalists, and some others of our group who had decided that wisdom encouraged a departure while that was still an option.

Three cars pulled away in the morning. We would see what few others had seen. There were burned out chassis of pickup trucks and buses along the side of the road. Hanging bridges were left from missile strikes.

At one point the three eastbound lanes had transformed into a huge bomb crater. There were US fighter jets in the air, and our drivers were convinced we would end up like the burnt chassis of other vehicles. We were moving very fast and the drivers had charged lots of money to take us out!

IT WAS AS THOUGH we had almost been able to stop a war. Five months had passed. Even early in November we were not sure Peggy Gish would be able to get in with the first CPT delegation before the war started. Then, for sure, it would start before Christmas. Then, it had to begin by the time the First Gulf War had lit up—January 15!

But, no! Still no war. Maybe the resistance around the world was bearing fruit. Could three mad men pull off a war alone? Certainly, before the shargee winds rained mud from the sky and blowing sand made tanks, M-16's, and helicopters grind to a halt, the war would have to start. But no. Maybe we had stopped a war! No, we had not.

We passed Rutbah, the only population center in the western desert. On a hanging bridge that had been hit by missiles, we passed a burned-out bus in the right lane. In the left lanes, I suspect we picked up shrapnel, which blew out our left rear tire about four kilometers west of town. We careened down a ditch, which would have been fine except there was a yawning hole at the end of the ditch.

The five of us in the car were injured. Those in the other two cars didn't look back for forty-five minutes, by which time they had reached the Jordanian border. The taxi with the Japanese journalists drove on. It took teammates in our other car some time to talk their driver into returning to that war zone, but he finally did.

We were pulling ourselves out of the destroyed car when an eastbound Iraqi driver stopped. He called across the median, "How can I help?" He loaded us into his vehicle and drove back into Rutbah with fighter jets still screaming through the air.

Those fighter jets were from the United States. In the past five months I had seen four Iraqi fighter jets. Usually it seemed their thunder, in sets of two over Baghdad, was to assure the population underneath that all was well. Those jets were all Iraq had and they did not appear when the active fighting started. It was less than a third-world military after the war with Iran and then the First Gulf War, followed by the vice of crushing economic sanctions for thirteen years.

Our helper took us to a small first aid station. Health responders put us on tables and took care of us. "It doesn't matter whether you are Iraqi or

American, we will take care of you." I don't think there was any question which category we were in.

The driver of the now destroyed car was an Iraqi. The young man on my right in the back seat was a Korean, Bae Sang Hyun, a peacemaker who had joined our group in Baghdad. Shane Claiborne was an evangelical activist from the Simple Way Community in the slums of Philly, and he sat on my left. Weldon Nisly was a Mennonite pastor from Seattle and had been in the passenger seat. I was an Indiana farmer in the middle of the back seat. My skull had etched into it the shape of the dome light which had essentially scalped me because there had been no seat belt. I clamped my CPT hat down hard to staunch the freely flowing blood.

"It doesn't matter whether you are Muslim or Christian. We will help you." That categorization would have been a bit more difficult this time, but I would guess they had some pretty quick assumptions. They seemed to be doing triage, caring for those most likely to survive first. The driver was least hurt except he had lost a car! My Korean companion was just banged up by the crash. Shane had a dislocated shoulder which was now in a sling. Weldon was getting a drip solution, had broken ribs and probably a broken collar bone. He was hurting pretty bad.

When they got to me, the doctor explained that US fighter jets had destroyed his children's hospital in Rutbah three days ago. A light bulb went on in my wounded head, so to speak. I was from the same country as the pilot of that fighter jet. I was the "enemy." The doctor proceeded to sew my head back together. I am alive today because someone who could have seen me as "enemy" saved my life.

JESUS HAD TOLD THE dramatic story of the Good Samaritan (Luke 10:29–36). The one who helped patch up the Jewish victim whom the robbers had left by the side of the road was not a good Jew. He was a hated Samaritan. I was not the Good Samaritan in this story. The good person was again an "enemy," the Iraqi doctor!

He also served as a good peacemaker—better than the peacemaker I was! I had not stopped the war against his good country, but here he was building strong bridges to the enemy nation. The same nation that had destroyed his bridges, on the three-hundred-mile-long, six-lane, divided highway going to Jordan. At that time, we had nothing like that highway or those bridges in my country, either physically or metaphorically.

Ever eat humble pie? Weren't we supposed to be the well-trained peacemakers? We had lots of experience. I'm not sure whether these medical personnel even had peacemaker training, but here they were showing up this peace team that had come to Iraq! One important part of peacemaking is to understand that we as peacemakers only hold a few of the puzzle pieces. Others will be carrying the rest of the pieces. We need to be graceful enough to see that it may be those whom we would least expect that will carry the biggest load in building peace.

Chapter 12

Great Expectations

IN JANUARY 2010, A small group of us went back into Rutbah, Iraq, as part of Greg Barrett's writing of the story of Rutbah. See *The Gospel of Rutba* published by Orbis Press. It was nearly seven years after the events of our Good Samaritan story.

Fear drives our world. Worry tries to protect our abundance from those we know have less than what we have. Stories we see on the evening news train our imaginations. Terror builds from the propaganda that benefits those who receive status or income wealth from vastly expanded "national security" programs. The unknown characteristics about those who are in some way different from us—skin color, religion, country of origin, gender, class, and orientation—dominate our emotions. These fears radically influence our daily decisions, usually forcing us in directions that rational thinking would avoid.

The two taxis we had taken from Amman, Jordan, were not allowed to carry us to the Iraqi border crossing because they did not have the proper licensing. We caught a ride finally in the back of a pickup, and received the proper stamps to proceed, but a Jordanian Major decided it was not safe for us to go into Iraq. He held us up until US Captain William Foster met us in the empty space between the Jordanian and Iraqi checkpoint crossings.

Both the Major and the Captain were armed and convinced that if we continued we would face either kidnapping or death, likely both in that order. Their perspective was probably shaped by the images of Anbar province that dominated the news. The reports from Anbar were usually of resistance attacks against internationals, actions against the Iraqi government, or general unrest.

As a CPTer, I had crossed through Anbar Province ten times, usually by car or bus. Only once did I travel by air because teammates had set different travel standards on the heels of a bombing in Baghdad against one of our NGO colleagues and her office complex. Certainly, there had been times when I had been uncertain how the trip would go but, except for the accident in 2003 during the US invasion, the trips had gone without negative incidents.

Once, by bus, Iraqi passengers had welcomed me and offered travel advice. Another time, Peggy Gish and Anne Montgomery were traveling with me on a trip to take back the space we had earlier conceded to the actors of violence, and our CPT vehicle was stopped at an Iraqi military checkpoint. It appeared they were not going to let us through because of our US passports. We bluffed our way through, saying, "It is really okay. There will be no problem."

"Are you sure?"

"Yes, everything will be fine."

Our driver set the speed control to 100 mph and often tailgated another car. He explained that if an IED (improvised explosive device) hit us, we were safer like this! To pass a US military convoy that stretched for miles, we crossed the median. The alternative, to pass the convoy on the three lanes going west was likely to result in a shooting by US guards that would cut short our own westward movement.

Weaving through oncoming traffic in the eastbound lanes at high speed was the most dangerous act of our trip to Jordan that time! Generally, our interactions with Iraqis and other travelers on that and other trips were very hospitable. The welcome and care that confronted us after the accident leaving Baghdad in 2003 was the standard fare of hospitality in our interactions with Iraqis, so I anticipated no problem in crossing this border in 2010 and going to Rutbah!

The Major and the Captain maintained their discouraging posture toward our crossing into Iraq. At some point an Iraqi officer drove up to our dialogue circle in a pickup truck. I noticed he was carrying no side arm so asked, "How is the travel to Rutbah? Will we have any troubles on that route?"

He queried, "Who is inviting you there?"

We explained that the mayor's office and the medical personnel at the hospital would be our hosts and that friends were coming to pick us up. He assured us that there would be no problem for us on such a trip and welcomed us to join him in his pickup to go on to the Iraqi border crossing.

Later in his office, as other Iraqi border personnel kept wandering in out of curiosity, Sami Rasouli expanded on the nature and work of Christian Peacemaker Teams and the Muslim Peacemaker Team (see chapter 6). The Iraqi border officers wanted to sign up!

Sami was our translator and "travel agent" for this short trip into Iraq. He had been in the initial training in Kerbala that CPT had done with a group of Iraqis in January 2005, a group that chose to become MPT.

At the entry checkpoint into Rutbah, one of the guards was duded up almost like a US soldier and had to play out his dramatic macho act. After what seemed like a long wait an escort vehicle arrived and led us on to the hospital.

In Rutbah itself, we settled into what were probably medical staff rooms at the hospital complex. Quickly after that we followed our hosts across the street to the mayor's office where we had a more formal welcome to the city. Yes, we were unusual faces in that city, and at least some of our hosts were quite concerned for our safety.

I WONDER HOW OUR expectations influence reality. I remember coming into Iraq my first time with Kathy Kelly after she had been on numerous trips there already during the 1990's. Her warm welcome into Iraq time after time had set the stage for me to expect the same. Yet the US State Department warned against such travel, threatening sanctions of huge fines and long imprisonment against us for counter actions.

Lt Col Nate Sassaman in Balad was sure it was unsafe for CPT to go into Abu Hishma village. But our invitation at the gate of the town from the middle of an unruly crowd seemed sufficient to take the risk to spend the night. Do our expectations set the parameters of what we will in fact experience?

I am sure that is true and set my expectations high in that light.

Chapter 13

Suicide Bomber Visits CPT

It is a fact that increased attacks against reported terrorist targets lead to innocent civilian deaths. This results in an increase in the resistance and those willing to become suicide bombers. Are there ways to counter these irresponsible actions by both sides? Let me share some stories.

Our CPT team was based in Baghdad in 2005. One afternoon, my Canadian CPT teammate, Stewart Vriesinga, was down at the market purchasing food to prepare for supper. It was his turn in the regular meal preparation rotation we had. Two young men accosted him with a list of names. CPT had been offering to help Iraqi families whose members the US occupation had arrested. Many of the families did not know where their family members were being held, what the charges against them were, or how they could visit. These two young men wanted CPT help with their list of names.

Stewart invited them to come to the CPT apartment after our meal, team meeting, and worship. So, near to 9 p.m., there was a knock on the door. We invited them in and shared tea around, an act of hospitality in Iraq. About five minutes into the conversation, the one who spoke English more fluently asked us all to set our tea cups down. He reached into his vest and pulled out a gun, saying, "Please remain calm. We are here on a mission to take out this house and everyone in it." He asked his friend to open his shirt. He was strapped with explosives. "The bomb goes off in fifteen minutes," he said.

I was sitting between the two on the couch. Sure, I madly contemplated sweeping them both into my crushing embrace to avert the catastrophe, but wisely chose to remain calm. They proceeded to tie us three men up and had the two women sit over on the couch. Then, with a hesitation the spokesperson said, "There may be a way out of this. Please go get team cash."

Jane McKay Wright, from Ontario, Canada, and tasked with our CPT accounts, left the room and came back with a stash of cash. Our visitor counted it, and said, "Not enough!"

Jim Loney remembered that he had $70 in his sock drawer. So, he and the man who was strapped, now flashing a six-inch knife through the air threatening Jim's ear, went to Jim's bedroom.

They couldn't find the cash, but when they returned, the other visitor was asking Peggy Gish to empty her backpack. They loaded in two cell phones, a digital camera, and a computer. As they backed out the door, the English speaker said, "Don't make any phone calls; you may yet get out of this alive."

Two guards across the street chased them for two blocks, but they escaped. As a team, we spent the next two hours debriefing. The event was not totally unexpected. Most other international NGOs (non-governmental organizations) had left Iraq. A friend, Margaret Hassan, from CARE, had suffered the bombing of her NGO office. A hostile group later kidnapped and killed her.

Why are we alive? Did we respond differently? Was it just a cover for a robbery? Did we have nonviolent tools of which we were unaware?

HERE IS ANOTHER STORY. A small CPT delegation in November 2005, had just visited Sunni religious offices in the western part of Baghdad. As the delegation drove out of the parking lot, two cars cut them off. Four CPTers—Tom Fox, Jim Loney, Harmeet Sooden, and Norman Kember— were whisked into another vehicle and taken as hostages. Their hosts issued demands in exchange for their release and held them for 118 days. Near the end of that time, Tom Fox was seemingly taken away to be released, but was found killed in western Baghdad.

Jim Loney shared two stories that struck me deeply from their time of captivity. The four CPTers were usually handcuffed to each other, and the end person would be tied to a door or a larger piece of furniture to prevent an escape like a jump from a window. Each evening guards unshackled them so they could use the toilet and granted them an opportunity to exercise. One evening Uncle, one of the hosts who was a huge man with massive arms and legs, had recently come back from a time away. He was sporting an even larger ankle, now sprained, injured maybe while playing soccer.

He was sitting in a chair when the CPTers were released. Tom took the opportunity to kneel at his feet and pray for the healing of his sprained ankle.

Junior was another of the hosts. His entire family had been killed during the US assault on Fallujah about a year earlier. He had frequent bouts of headaches and muscle tightness. CPTers were sure that, if things blew up, Junior would be the source of the explosion. During another evening release, Jim approached Junior and began to massage his shoulders. Jim recounts that Junior melted in his hands. No one had ever touched Junior like that before.

It was not long after these events that someone contacted a Canadian consulate person saying he could take the consul to the CPTers. A deal was worked out that the hosts would be given fifteen minutes to leave before British Special Forces moved in to release the hostages.

The scripture in Acts 9:1–19 tells the story of the transformations of Saul/ Paul and Ananias. They were intense enemies brought into unexpected contact with each other by the Spirit of Jesus. That contact changed both of them in unexpected ways and led to consequences that no one would have believed possible.

It may be that the security we long for in what seems to be a most dangerous world has its source in our most difficult antagonist. If we are willing to break through those boxes of "enemy," an entirely different future may open up.

Here is a third story. Lieutenant Colonel Nate Sassaman was the commanding officer at US Paliwoda Forward Operating Base in Balad, about an hour north of Baghdad. Through working relationships with Iraqi human rights lawyers, CPT had regular contact with Nate. Journalists who were friends of CPT asked CPT to facilitate an opportunity to embed with Nate's troops. We entered the base and made the request only to learn that Nate was headed out on a mission and wouldn't be able to meet with us.

We were talking with guards at the entrance when, sure enough, a convoy of tanks and humvees swept past us and a cloud of dust rolled over us. Abruptly the line of vehicles came to a halt and a man crawled out of the lead Abrams tank. "Kindy, I want to talk with you!"

"Well, sure enough, Nate, we want to talk with you too!"

"Cliff, we are worried about you CPTers. You don't have armed guards, you ride in regular taxis, all in very dangerous territory. You could easily be kidnapped or killed. Here, why don't you try on my flak jacket?"

Nate had played quarterback when Army took the national title so we were a bit different in size, but I shrugged off my backpack and slipped into his flak jacket.

"You know, Nate, you don't understand. We have a different way of developing security. We try to build friendships and use those relationships as a basis for our long-term sustainable security. In fact, we have an open bedroom back at our apartment. Why don't you join CPT for a time? You would find a whole different window on this country from what you have riding in that tank.

"You couldn't bring that tank to our CPT apartment because we don't have a place to park it; we don't allow guns in the house, so you would have to leave behind your M-16; and you might choose to leave this flak jacket because it will make you so visible and vulnerable. Would you be willing to explore this different perspective?" I asked.

Nate paused, adding, "I need to check with my wife first, and I'm only a few months away from drawing a full pension."

As far as I know Nate never did follow up on that invitation. It is clear that our CPT way of relating in that "dangerous" region did provide a different kind and level of safety from that which Nate and his troops had achieved.

Nate had surrounded Abu Hishma Village with razor wire, instituted a total curfew, and controlled the entrance and exit of any villagers. This happened because one of his units had been fired upon, and one of the men killed, while driving one of the roads near Abu Hishma. Iraqi human rights lawyers encouraged us to visit the village.

CPT took a delegation there. Villagers surrounded us. Soon one father was screaming at me about his son who had been killed by US forces. I began to feel I had taken this delegation into a very insecure location, perhaps fatally so.

Suddenly someone tugged on me from the other side, "Why don't you come and stay in our village?"

"You mean overnight?"

"Yes."

I turned to ask one of my teammates for her thoughts and found the previously screaming father smiling and offering me a cigarette.

Later, Nate strongly discouraged such a visit, but CPT carefully planned for a few from our team to visit and for the others to stay in nearby Balad at a secure hotel. Our plans disintegrated when curfew caught us all inside the village. Our inviting party, a journalist, was not at home that day as he had planned to be. His young son took us to a neighbor's home. This neighbor turned out to be the chief of a forty-thousand-member tribe. His family welcomed us strangers off the street, fed us, provided warm hospitality, and secured us for the night. Tradition has it that once a guest eats at the table of a desert family, that guest can expect to be provided security from any dangers.

We toured the village the next day. At one place a US tomahawk missile had blown up the income-providing orchard of a family. Where homes had been demolished by US air attacks and we were taking pictures, we were confronted with US helicopter gunships flying overhead. Villagers told stories of soldiers hanging out the doors of the gunships randomly spraying live fire at villagers below.

The stories got worse. Such actions were among those that destroyed the tentatively good relationships that US personnel had immediately after their March 2003 invasion. Those so-called tools of security, tomahawk missiles and helicopter gunships, only worsened the security situation for both Iraqis and Americans.

Chapter 14

War by Corporation, Globalized

POLITICAL PARTIES SEEM TO dominate much of the discussion taking place across the United States at this time in 2020. A divide between blue and red states, or Democratic and Republican parties, appears to set the stage for any dialogue to be less than civil. I wonder if there might not be common themes that, in fact, provide some unity in understanding our living together.

North Manchester is a small rural community with mostly middle and lower-class folks, if we look at education, income, and availability of choices compared to the rest of the country. At this point our local economy is impacted more by decisions made hundreds or thousands of miles outside our region than by decisions made in our own homes and offices.

Agriculture is an important segment of this local economy. Prices for soybeans and corn are set by markets with little influence from our local fields. What can be grown for markets seems to be dictated elsewhere. Cost of equipment and farming inputs like seeds, fertilizer, and chemicals are not decisions we make. We do provide the labor and take out the loans, but we do not control the weather that impacts the harvest or the monetary policy of the banks. Looking at some economic realities might help us ground our opinions and actions more in accord with their impact on our lives.

For example, the people of the United States have recently come out of one of the more difficult economic periods we have ever faced, while corporations are reporting some of the most lucrative quarters in their income history. The middle class is dwindling here in our country. The divide between the most wealthy and those who are in the lower segment of the economic spectrum is larger than it has ever been.

In my travel and work around the world responding to disasters or developing peaceful ways to deal with conflict situations, I have seen many US experiments with privatization. The Pentagon is hiring private contractors, usually part of large corporations, at hugely higher costs to do jobs that the US military personnel used to do. That privatization is happening also in prisons, education, infrastructure, disaster response, and social services. One of the consequences of privatization is a massive transfer of public wealth to corporate wealth. Privatization may be more accurately called piratization, since most people do not get a share of this "private" wealth.

An additional cost of privatization is the lack of accountability that comes with this transfer of wealth. Private contractors do not have the same responsibility to the citizens that those who have been part of the hiring/firing structures of government do. There are no records of where the money went for some of the major corporate contracts related to the Iraq and Afghanistan wars. The United States also has been forced to cover for private contractors who have acted outside the policies of the war and essentially dragged our government in directions which it had not chosen to go.

Remember that corporations have been seen by the US courts as individuals with the accompanying rights. Those corporations are glad to utilize those rights and receive tax write offs and incentives from all different levels of government in exchange for locating in a state. But then, because their bottom line is profit for investors, they freely move out of the country if they find cheaper labor, lower tax rates, or lower environmental standards that allow for greater profit. They become stateless in their ability to manipulate incentives, employment, and environmental policies to their benefit. The impact their decisions have on our communities is not their concern. Sure, they must have some level of concern for decent public relations, but the bottom line remains the dollar. The benefits of their statelessness and utilization, in the courts of individual rights, grant them virtual impunity when any political entity tries to hold them accountable for the negative consequences of their actions.

If I understand correctly, their existence is dependent upon our initial public granting of their incorporation charter. That has not seemed to carry with it any continuing responsibility to our society. We are in a period during which corporations and the richest people in our society are receiving major tax cuts. Communities are offering major incentives to attract corporations to settle in their locale. Yet I heard of a solar panel corporation in Connecticut which had accepted huge incentives to settle there. They hired eight hundred employees. Not long after that they made the decision to move to China, leaving behind the employees and the state. The bottom line of profit determines the decision and human beings and the good of society become minor factors.

TAKE A DEEPER STEP with me. Elections are dominated by corporate money. The US Supreme Court has opened doors to major corporate campaign funding with no requirement to report those contributions in a public fashion. How will money impact legislation that comes from the legislators bought with those monies?

Check out wars. Iraq, Afghanistan, and Syria have made many losers, among them the people of Iraq, Afghanistan, and Syria. The cost of the first two wars is in the trillions of dollars. Additionally, US military personnel have been the losers; they have had to pay the deep personal costs of war, including post-traumatic stress, suicides, brain injuries, family breakups, unemployment, and homelessness. The United States has been the loser. The image of the US has plummeted on the world stage because the wars have bankrupted us and decimated our image across the globe.

So why do we go to war? Does someone benefit? Sure! A president gets elected with a commitment to end one war. Once in office, his words change. What has brought the change? Who pushes and pulls? Often military leaders are reluctant to go to war. Who are the beneficiaries of war that push a country into those policies of war?

Corporations make lots of money on war. It was true during the major world wars of the last century. Especially now as expensive tools and machinery are the big costs of war, corporations make more money when wars are extended. Their lobbyists have ready access to the offices of Representatives and Senators, especially as they spread out their largess into the various legislative districts across the country. Munitions companies are ecstatic about the increase in violence across the globe. The prospects for more military contracts are on their doorsteps!

When federal budgets are being slashed, which budgets will be protected? The Pentagon budget kept on growing as the Cold War ended. The United States became the world's lone superpower, as the military budget from our country matched the total military expenditures of the rest of the world. Security is based solely on expenditures for military might. There is no concern for the education of our children and no worry about collapsing bridges. Here we have roads filled with as many potholes as the roads in the war zones of the world. In our country, there is no concern about a health care system that fills the pockets of insurance companies and medical supply corporations and drags our national health ranking down to thirty-seventh place in the World Health Organization lineup of healthy countries. We have security from what and for what?

And for export? We sell more weapons than any other country in the world. They are one of our major exports. Those exports help to balance our fiscal budget. At whose expense? We are presently at war in Iraq, Afghanistan, Yemen, Pakistan, Syria, and Somalia. The citizens of those countries and the fighters we send to those wars are bearing the costs. We would be seen by any clear minded person as a military state.

A nation at war is a nation afraid. What do we fear? Does any perceived threat to our high style of living require other countries to give up even a simple standard of living? Is it fear of losing access to the resources that fuel our corporations? Are corporations complicit in driving the engines of war? Is justification laid out that a gullible public will buy, in order to continue paying its taxes for war and offering up its sons and daughters as the sacrifices to the gods of money and war? Do the revolving doors between lax government oversight and corporate feeding at the troughs of Pentagon funding expose military sickness?

Anyone who exposes the truth is seen as a threat. When WikiLeaks released the videos of US helicopter gunships knowingly killing unarmed civilians stopping to help after an accident in Afghanistan, the world was appalled. But the federal government wants to charge those who might be involved in the leaked videos with treason. Homeland Security has its eyes and ears inside our computers, cell phones, email messages, on our public streets, and yet they say that any call for openness and accountability on their part is uncalled for?!

A political democracy depends on transparency and openness of information. If the public is to make sound decisions, it needs access to the data that impact decisions. Corporations that expect the benefits of corporate status, without the balancing responsibilities to the community, destroy a healthy society. Especially when those deceits can be covered up by bought media and purchased politicians, it is difficult for the electorate to make informed decisions. Corporations and their activities need to become a transparent window to earn their rightful place in society. If not, the public which granted those corporate charters must take them back.

Corporations are an excellent focus for plowsharing nonviolence campaigns. Moral activists must enlarge peacemaking strategies to engage war corporations in the boardrooms, investment portfolios, and employment lines. Churches and civil society could include corporate war-making in biblical sermons and social critiques and as a target of nonviolent actions for peace. Our involvements will take our actions into the resource-rich countries of the world.

Chapter 15

Wild Colombian Bulls

Four of us left for Colombia in January 2002. We were the exploratory team that would test whether Christian Peacemaker Teams should place a team in that country at the request of the Mennonite Church in Colombia. Land and wealth were held by a small minority of the population. Armed actors lined up on different sides of that justice struggle leading to the deaths of thousands and the migration of millions. Did CPT have a peacemaking role to play in Colombia?

Fortunately, Peace Brigades International and Witness for Peace had been in the country for some time and had good experience on the ground. Both of those highly capable organizations were clear, though, that CPT should continue the policy those two groups had started of not talking with armed actors. According to them, CPT should also use planes for in-country travel, rather than buses that could be stopped at checkpoints staffed by armed actors. If CPT started making connections with the paramilitary forces, for example, the FARC (Fuerzas Armadas Revolucionarias de Colombia) guerrilla resistance fighters would see CPT as enemies. FARC would then target CPTers for kidnapping or death—not exactly how we wanted to start our new project. If contacting FARC, CPT would be similarly targeted by the Colombian paramilitary.

Cristina Forand and I went to Putumayo in the south where paramilitaries and guerrillas fought over control of coca fields as a primary source of financing for their respective military operations. The United States funded Colombia to the tune of $3 billion per year to counter these drug scourges, and also provided counterinsurgency training for Colombian military personnel at the School of the Americas in Fort Benning, Georgia. The paramilitary started when large landowners felt vulnerable because of the guerrilla fighters and hired these private guns for protection. The paramilitary worked closely with the Colombian military and provided them an easily deniable route for murderous, illegal actions without accountability.

On the other hand, FARC had started in 1964 because of the huge economic divide between those few who owned land, and those many who had no land or money to sustain life in a country very rich in resources and land. FARC was like a Robin Hood gang, which over the next fifty years spiraled downward. They became a movement dependent on kidnapping, ransom demands, and growth of coca to fund deadly operations.

In Putumayo, US-funded planes sprayed many coca fields to stop the drug trade. Interestingly, there would be other huge coca fields just across the road that would not be touched with spray. Many communities suspected of having guerrilla sympathies would have their gardens, rivers, animals, and homes sprayed as well. It might have been good to place a team there, but local supporters and an indigenous nonviolence movement didn't seem ready to initiate a request and serve as our partners in that region.

We also did some exploring for a project setting in Nariño in the southwest of the country. In the far north, CPTer Duane Ediger tested the possibilities with an Afro-Colombian community. Again, in these settings the pieces of the puzzle did not quite come together for a project.

We began to gather some focus for a project in the area near Barrancabermeja while working closely with El Programa de Desarollo y Paz del Magdalena Medio (Programa), a Catholic peace and development organization. Another group we had met with, in Bogotá, invited CPT to send some volunteers to join them on a trek toward Cúcuta, in the northeast of the country close to Venezuela. This was a region where people were devastated by the violence, drowned by despair. CPT would be traveling with this group and a very creative dance team that wanted to use their artistic efforts to nurture nonviolence.

A friend, Sarah Rich, asks if art and creativity necessarily stimulate nonviolence. How would you respond to this question? Or does nonviolence stimulate art and creativity?

Striding on long stilts and dressed in long flowing garb, the dance troupe exploded into small communities that had been impacted heavily by the fighting. As they swept down the streets, that presence transformed people. I remember old grandparents sitting tiredly on stoops who would just dance with delight, and lethargic children who would bubble with joy and possibility at these wild scenes. In settings where hope was impossible, this small creative interjection made the future wide open again.

After travel that led through several villages, we were close to the Venezuelan border. Our Bogotá friends invited us to join them in returning home by plane. Janet Shoemaker and I got to the small airport with them, but they filled all fourteen seats in the tiny plane. There were no seats for the two of us CPTers. Our Bogotá friends did have a contact with the Catholic parish where we could spend the night. Early the next morning the priest was traveling south to where we could catch a bus. There seemed to be no other options, so we took this one. There were heightened tensions with the uncertainties of roadblocks, but we caught our bus. The bus was stopped at a checkpoint by armed actors, but this entailed no problem for us.

Not long after that incident, CPT moved into a house in Barrancabermeja. In fact, it was into a neighborhood that had just been taken over by paramilitaries from guerrillas. On one of the first nights, we ran into paramilitary patrols on the street. I think it was Duane Ediger who gathered us in a prayer circle, inviting them to join us in prayer for the people in this troubled region. Yes, they were quite uncomfortable, but we began to shape a possibility for dialogue with those carrying guns.

Near the end of those three months in Colombia, Cristina and I were in the community of Rio Nuevo Ité, west of the Magdalena River that flowed north from Barrancabermeja. We had been asked to live with that small village, as a protective presence in the face of joint Colombian military/paramilitary operations in the region, which had chased them into the mountains for two months. Janet Shoemaker and Duane Ediger were in the San Francisco community several hours downstream.

It was Palm Sunday afternoon. Cristina and I were playing chess in the heat of the shade outside the house when three riders on horseback pulled into the yard. They had heard about our accompaniment here in Rio Nuevo Ité and had ridden for three days to ask us to come and hold a similar role with their community up in the mountains to the west. Since we four CPTers were soon to leave the country, we told them we would tell Sandra who was our contact with Programa, the group with which we partnered.

When we did, she got excited. There had been reports of a chainsaw massacre of one hundred people by paramilitary fighters down in Nariño. The riders had reported paramilitary checkpoints, which prevented food and medicine from getting to the displacement camps where those fleeing the widespread violence in Antioquia State found some protection. Sandra asked,

"If I am able to get media representatives, some human rights folks, and some refugee workers, would CPT be willing to join that group for a few days?"

Duane and Janet would be gone by then and Cristina would be in Bogotá, so it didn't quite fit the definition of "Team" in Christian Peacemaker Teams. But since there would be others it did seem important for CPT to be part of this action, even if it appeared I would be the only CPTer available. Sandra came back with the news that none of the other groups could or wanted to go. Would I go by myself? Cristina and I talked.

"You know, when armed actors see an international person, they assume there are lots of others there with them. And our small presence in Rio Nuevo Ité really did make a dramatic difference even though there were five hundred military/paramilitary operating in that zone while we were there," she said. It wasn't the best way to go into Antioquia, and on to a displacement community. But it might work.

I took the bus upriver to Puerto Berrío, where I could catch another bus over dirt roads for six hours. I began to see homes that had been taken over by what appeared to be groups of military. Our bus was stopped at a military checkpoint, but the soldiers basically ignored me. One soldier was talking with the driver outside the bus when I remembered my teammates' counsel to always document my activity. I did have this nice digital camera.

As I snapped the picture, the soldier glanced up. He charged into the bus, and I spent the next half hour being interrogated by the squad. I was accused of stealing a bedsheet from the military because the one in my bedroll looked just like theirs! Eventually, as other passengers became more impatient, soldiers decided that I was probably just naive and innocent and let me get back on the bus.

Remedios and Segovia were two towns in the gold and coal mining region of this central highland. The streets were lined with shops that sold coal and sported signs, "We buy gold." There was a sprawling military base between the towns. When my bus arrived in Segovia, it was already mid-afternoon. According to locals, it was too dangerous to continue my trip because of paramilitary activity. I called Sandra and got her answering machine. I left a message that I was fine, would spend the night in Segovia, and would travel on the next day.

When she got the message, she called all the hotels she could find in Segovia in her phone book, but she couldn't find one with this gringo in it. She freaked out and called Cristina in Bogotá. The report began to go out that I had been "disappeared"—shorthand for being kidnapped, killed, or otherwise removed.

The next morning, I caught a four-wheel drive jeep to the end of the road where I thought I would find Carlos, one of the three riders we had met in Rio Nuevo Ité. This community at the end of the road was a lumber town, but there was no Carlos. Really, what did I expect? We hadn't been able to notify them that I was coming because there was no phone here.

I stopped at a bar where there were people around. "So, how do I get to Cristalina?"

"You see that big mountain and the trail up over it? That's how to get there."

"Well, I'd better get started."

"No! It's not safe."

"Is there another way?"

"No."

"Then I'd better get started."

In those first hours, I passed several abandoned camps. By the signs of their litter, they were probably military/paramilitary operations. Then I passed through a tiny hamlet that was totally abandoned, with paramilitary graffiti on the walls of the houses. Occasionally, I would pass a mule train hauling slabs of lumber out of the deep jungle. There would be one mule train driver and six to twelve mules with slabs of lumber roped tightly to the sides of each mule and dragging in the trail behind. They were my regular reassurances I was on the correct trail.

I ran out of clean drinking water and was not carrying much food, because I expected to be cared for by the three men who had talked with us in Rio Nuevo Ité. I cleared a rise and looked down over a beautiful valley with a ranch, cattle, and a river.

I could see someone with khaki clothing and assumed it might be paramilitary since they were usually connected to big ranchers. But I didn't have many options, so down I went. Partners Marta Restrepo and Andrés Perez were watching over the ranch for a grandfather who was ill. Andrés was gone for a bit, but Marta invited me to spend the night. My earlier question about the distance to Cristalina and whether I could reach it by nightfall was answered with a guffaw.

I don't mind meeting armed actors by daylight, but I wasn't anxious to meet an armed actor after dark when my presence might surprise them. Andrés soon returned and he offered me a horse. I was feeling good being on foot, because it presents a different image, one that is not so threatening to another person who might be suspicious. I declined his offer.

In the morning I awoke to find that other travelers had also spent the night at the ranch. In fact the father of Francisco, whom I was to meet in Cristalina, and two others had plans to travel on that day! The complication was that they planned to drive a herd of bulls back into the mountains. I was welcome to join them. The ranch caretaker again offered a horse and I acquiesced.

The herders caught two wild bulls, chained them neck to neck to two tame bulls, and we set off with about fifty bulls altogether. I was invited to lead the way. "No problem, just follow the trail."

My horse tacked back and forth on the trail as we climbed out of the valley. It was amazing! Water puddles surrounded by butterflies that I had only seen in picture books. There were trees with trunks big enough to span the width of my house back in Indiana. The birds would have added to my life birding list, had I been building one. My horse and I reached the top of the ridge far ahead of the bulls. I was enjoying this pristine beauty when I felt a shudder—like an earthquake, which I guess isn't too unexpected.

Then my horse took the bit in its teeth and bolted. The shudder was the stampede of bulls down the mountain. My horse hit a root and flipped. It landed on my leg and I was sure it was broken. I dragged myself after the horse into the lee of some trees and the herd passed.

My fellow travelers caught up. "Where are the bulls?"

"I may have a broken leg and I'm not sure if my horse is okay."

"Forget the horse. Where are the bulls?"

I clambered onto the horse; they thought it was fine. The advantage I gained was that I was trailing the herd now instead of leading the way.

Further down the trail, two bulls gamboled into the jungle. We had to circle up the herd, with me holding in the rear position, while two men went in after the bulls. Then, of all things, seven other bulls crashed off into the jungle on the other side of the trail!

I looked around. Kryss Chupp never took us through this kind of training for CPT! I dropped the reins and dismounted to head into the jungle. The vines wrapped around me like anaconda snakes and I stumbled into a huge pit. But I finally found the bulls, probably at the point they figured they were lost. I yelled and heard my voice echo through the trees. No answer. "Great! Lost in the Colombian jungle!"

The bulls worked their way out on a tiny track and I followed. We came out onto the main trail just as the other men came out with their two captive bulls. "What happened? How did you get these seven bulls back out?" they asked.

"I don't know, but they are all yours," I replied.

Not too far down the trail the others stopped to eat. My time seemed to be running out faster than the hours I had before I needed to be back. I decided to go on ahead without my companions.

"It's easy. Just three clearings to go."

IT WAS MUCH AS I imagine Indiana would have been in the early 1800s, a few clearings surrounded with huge trees and this one tiny trail winding up the mountains and through the valleys. There was lots of distance between clearings.

I reached what I assumed was Cristalina. My throaty holler yielded no response, so I went on until I met another traveler who assured me that my first guess was correct. I returned and called again to find an ecstatic welcome from Francisco. He was happy to see me, but amazed I had come alone. He was ready to go on to the refugee camp immediately, but his wife's caution about dangerous trails with armed actors changed his mind.

"Okay, we'll get up early, saddle the horses, and hit the trail long before daybreak," Francisco said, "Do you have a flashlight?"

My mind walked back over the path on which I had just come in, trees down across the trail and my horse easing its way past the downed tree with a seventy-foot chasm dropping from the edge of the trail. Now I was going to retrace the route, but in the dark, with a tiny flashlight?!

We woke the roosters, maneuvered the tricky trail, and ran into Carlos before dawn. Later we met a FARC guerrilla fighter, alone. About eight o'clock, just after we had gathered the third of the original three riders into Rio Nuevo Ité, we pulled into the refugee camp. The displaced families were excited. Finally, someone had heard of their plight and had come to be with them. We met over breakfast and I commiserated with their stories.

They understood the difficulty of reaching this site, but there was another way back. First, they took me past the school building. Paramilitary at checkpoints had turned back their teacher. Just a month earlier, paramilitary had killed the husband of one of the committee members who was leading me. She stopped and picked a rose bud. "Cliff, this is a symbol of the trust we are placing in you. The world needs to know our plight and send help. We trust you to carry this news." My shoulders sagged under this added burden of expectation.

They took me on past the school to higher ground. "We could clear this brush with machetes and visitors could land here with a helicopter."

"Yes, you are right. I will carry the message out and we will trust this can happen as planned."

Back in the camp, a fresh horse appeared. Someone at the camp pointed me toward the shortcut back to the town at the end of the driving road. I rode hard hoping to arrive in time to catch a logging truck out. No such luck. The ranch caretakers were in town, though, and they again offered me a bed. "There is a milk truck that leaves a dairy farm at 7 a.m. That farm is about two hours away by foot."

I was up before five and pushed hard. I arrived well before 7:00, but the milk truck was already gone. Hitchhiking was slow, but I finally got a car ride back into Segovia in time to catch the bus. The military checkpoint was still in place but they ignored me this time. I arrived back at Sandra's office after dark. She was very glad to find me un-disappeared!

We made a plan. Sandra would contact Colombian human rights groups and media. Back in the United States I would contact the International Committee of the Red Cross and the United Nations High Commissioner for Refugees. Eight months later, there were still no problems reported from this displaced community in the conflict zone of Antioquia State in Colombia. Nonviolent gambles can pay off.

Chapter 16

Violence to Nonviolence

CROSSING LINES WORKS. OUR images of those on the other side of the barriers we build between one another are quite skewed. To be able to put a human face on those we call "enemy" is an important step. How should "enemy" be defined? Is "enemy" the person or group that threatens the life or existence of humanity in general, or me and my group in particular?

In Iraq in 2005, CPT had just finished training the Muslim Peace-maker Team (MPT) in Kerbala, about an hour and a half south of Baghdad. Hussein al Ibrihimi, our contact with MPT, reminded me there was another group that wanted to talk with us.

We checked with our translators. We needed good translation going into this meeting. They refused, "These people are off the wall. There is no way we would go with you."

We figuratively twisted arms and finally got one to agree to go with us—glumly, as if to say, "Okay, I'll go die with you."

Two representatives of Muqtada al-Sadr met with Peggy Gish and me. Al-Sadr is the so-called firebrand Shia cleric who, as an Iraqi nationalist, wanted all US troops out of the country. One of his representatives that day was a high school teacher and the other was a veterinarian. They were nicely dressed and quite congenial. Their question? "Tell us about nonviolence. We have and know how to use the tools of violence, but sometimes they don't work. Tell us about nonviolence."

Al Sadr's group carried out some of the most dramatic nonviolent actions I saw in Iraq. An early one was a demonstration at the Oil Ministry, one of the most closely guarded locations following the US invasion. The demonstration was about the unemployment that plagued Iraq. If people had jobs, they wouldn't hire on with the resistance just to be able to support their families—at $100 a strike against an American target

After our meeting, al-Sadr's group participated in two other non-violent actions that caught my attention. At that time, there were gas lines, twenty-four to forty-eight hours long, all across Iraq. Armed Iraqi soldiers and US military tanks intervened to speed the lines, but to no avail. In Sadr City, where al-Sadr's people were responsible for security, the lines were the same. Sadr's unarmed activists stepped in to stop black marketers who bought plastic jugs of gasoline to sell half a mile down the street at a higher price. The activists helped to reconcile arguments when drivers pulled in front of other drivers who had fallen asleep. Soon there were no gas lines in Sadr City!

Again, when Tel Afar was blockaded by US troops, Sadr's group organized a caravan to carry water, food, and medicine to the people inside the blockade. CPTers accompanied this caravan. If the US had responded positively to this nonviolence, the war in Iraq might have gone very differently. This brand of Iraqi nationalism was much different from the US-approved political leadership that gave Iran new leverage in the Middle East.

NOTE WITH ME THAT *crossing the barriers that grow up between people can transform both parties. In this instance, we opened our eyes to see that violent actors had the potential to be some of the most creative and successful nonviolent actors. Al-Sadr's people dared to approach a group, most of whom were from the United States, with the expectation that folks from that group might have some helpful answers for them.*

How do folks change from being actors of violence to becoming actors of nonviolence? In my work and living, I have interacted with many people who once were avid warriors. Their exposure to a different side of the picture—during or after the war—flipped their commitment to one of peacemaking. I don't know that I have met or worked with those who have flipped the other way. I expect an experience of grave injustice, where an individual saw no other way to try to correct the injustice, might drive her/him to violence. It behooves peacemakers to teach others about the many nonviolent tools we carry in our tool bags!

Chapter 17

Mayan Abejas Nonviolence

A CHRISTIAN PEACEMAKER TEAM delegation was in the displacement community of Xoyép just before the massacre of forty-five indigenous nonviolent Mayan villagers known as Las Abejas, or The Bees. Armed paramilitary slaughtered them on a raid into the nearby village of Acteál. Fray Bartolomé de las Casas, the human rights arm of the Catholic Church under Archbishop Samuel Ruiz, invited CPT to come back to that embattled region of southern Mexico.

An exploratory team of four of us did go in 1998. It was a difficult assignment, since about three hundred internationals had just been evicted from the country for doing the kinds of things we proposed to do. Military and immigration checkpoints were the enforcement structures that restrained travelers from going into Chenalhó Municipality, Chiapas State. Chenalhó was, as a jurisdiction, like a county in the US. It was about 97% indigenous Mayan, about 70% of whom had been moved from their homes into displacement communities where they found a tiny semblance of security.

The armed Zapatista uprising there, and a bit further east, had sparked a strong military presence. There were twenty-one Mexican military bases scattered throughout Chenalhó Municipality. It seemed clear that the attack on Acteál had been carried out by paramilitary units but with strong support from the Mexican military. The paramilitary nature of the operation granted some deniability to the government responsibility.

In order to avoid what appeared to be the most likely exit route for our CPT unit, we began early on to stop and pray at the checkpoints. We would pray before the staff had the opportunity to start interrogating us about our presence in the region. We always invited those staffing the checkpoint to join us in prayer for the highlands. Our prayers would include the hope that these military and immigration staff could return home so that the Mayan communities could also go home. Before long, staff would see us coming and disappear into, or behind, their shelter. Soon the immigration checkpoints were pulled from those roads entering Chenalhó Municipality.

Living situations in displacement camps like Acteál and Xoyép were quite trying. Food was often in short supply, sanitary conditions were difficult, medical care was lacking, and education for children was minimal.

Las Abejas, The Bees, was the organizational structure for the displacement communities. The image of working together for the good of the hive was one that easily translated into their context. It was majority Catholic, but also included many Protestant and traditional Mayan faith members who worked fairly smoothly across those faith lines. The directing group met regularly to focus on the concerns of the communities and initiate actions for the betterment of the "hive."

During CPT's time there, the camps started gardens, trained teachers, built composting toilets, managed water collection systems, developed a network of medical practitioners, and improved the temporary housing shelters. They also gathered for worship regularly, planted corn on the helicopter landing pad at a nearby military base, celebrated, and held off invading military units that encroached on displacement land. During holy seasons like Lent, they carried out extensive liturgical actions that connected the stations of the cross to a series of activities and marches encouraging the military bases to leave or close.

CPT joined and assisted in some of those activities. These became steps of empowerment for the displaced families. Doctors without Borders, European accompaniment groups, and regular visits from the Archbishop and his entourage were also part of the energizing recipe.

It was during this period that NAFTA (the North American Free Trade Agreement) fell like a smothering straight jacket on the southern portion of the continent. Under NAFTA, Mexican farmers no longer could receive government subsidies for growing corn, the lifeline of Mayan culture and the staple of the country. So, subsidized US corn sold more cheaply in the markets of Mexico than the locally grown grain. Coffee, the other prominent crop of this mountainous zone, went from twenty four to eight pesos per kilogram on the global markets.

This was a double disaster for the majority farming population of Chiapas. This disaster engulfed the Las Abejas communities too. Not that they were not good farmers! Anyone who can grow crops and survive on the seventy-degree slopes that comprise Chenalhó Municipality has farming expertise.

Over the next few years about three million men and boys from Chiapas made the hard decision to go north across the border for jobs because they could no longer provide a living for their families by farming in Chiapas. They left, not by choice, but by necessity. However, Las Abejas communities, perhaps because they focused on the health of the hive, somehow survived and stayed together.

They started organic cooperatives for coffee. They expanded sustainable practices like starting short retaining bushes on the downhill side of coffee plants. Those short shrubs caught the leaves and roiling rain that tried to erode the steep slopes. Shade grown coffee was natural for them already. Adaptability and intentional planning by the collective enabled Abejas families to stay together.

CPT teams spent much of those four years living in the camps with Abejas families. Sometimes meals were meager, with watered down beans, a single hot pepper, tortillas, and weak coffee. I remember laying on my wooden bed in my sleeping bag in the Acteál camp with a drip of rain coming through a small hole in the roof over my bunk. It was a nuisance until I figured out that it was a bullet hole from the earlier massacre here in this same community.

Military pressure, intending to move the Abejas from this municipality to urban areas elsewhere, did not succeed. Pharmaceutical companies wanted to discover and patent the life forms that were prominent in the jungles and used by the indigenous people. Foreign companies wanted to flood these mountain valleys for the water that could be exported. There was talk of a wide superhighway to compete with the Panama Canal for the movement of goods from one ocean trade zone to the other. As in other countries like ours, the indigenous people were expected to move on and leave anything of value behind for others.

The Abejas were different. I don't know if they even knew the term "constructive program," but they were nonviolently living Badshah Khan's resistance to violence and injustice, while building a sustainable economic society on the rubble of what had been.

They had discovered new niches for farming and making a living. Their unity provided strength. They had developed a strong infrastructure of health care, education, and skills to pass on to the next generation. Their experiments became models for neighboring communities also struggling with dramatic changes. At the end of our four years of ac-companying Las Abejas, most of the displaced communities had returned to their home villages much stronger, prepared to survive in changing political times.

Chapter 18

Campaign in Vieques, Puerto Rico

IN MAY 2000, US Coast Guard ships and a destroyer had stopped all sea traffic going to the east end of Vieques, Puerto Rico. Two thousand troops from Fort Bragg, North Carolina, were waiting on transport ships, ready to come ashore as needed. Other troops and security were already on land, cutting off land routes back to the middle of Vieques. FBI and US Federal Marshals were coming down from the many helicopters whirling through the air. A purple helicopter, which appeared to be the command ship, circled the beaches below. Two hundred sixteen women and men faced immediate arrest for establishing nonviolent peace encampments in the bombing zone at the east end of the island of Vieques.

After decades of struggle by the fishers of Vieques to recover their prime fishing spots from the US Navy, seven camps had been set up by various resistance groups in January 2000. The presence of those camps had halted the nearly constant bombardment of that bombing zone. Those aerial attacks had made this land one of the most heavily bombed sites in the world.

But I am getting ahead of myself! This Vieques Island, part of Puerto Rico, was the home of civilians who eked out a living in small scattered communities. It had some of the clearest archaeological sites of an older people, the Taíno, who had lived here before Columbus sailed into nearby waters.

DURING THE SECOND WORLD War, the US military confiscated this area. ($50 for six acres of sugarcane and potatoes, along with a bulldozed family home, does not qualify as a purchase.) It would become a training ground and bombing zone to prepare troops for the battlefields of Europe and Asia, and later, Vietnam and Iraq. Munitions manufacturers used the bombing zone to test their weapons.

The deep offshore waters allowed nuclear-powered submarines to blast away at this small target. Battleships could anchor offshore and level heavy ordnance from their big guns onto the land. A long, clear, seventy-mile air corridor to the east facilitated assaults on the target by fighter jets and heavily loaded bombers. The beaches were ideal for landing ships to disgorge their hordes of fighting troops onto the unsuspecting island. The west third of the island was trenched with mammoth munitions bunkers. The people lived in the middle.

The constant bombardment included concentrations of heavy metals from the exploding munitions. Lead, cadmium, beryllium, arsenic, barium, boron, cyanide, mercury, hexavalent chromium, agent orange, napalm, and even depleted uranium in later years spread their toxic wares across the land and into the waters. Fish could not survive; cancer and leukemia rates rose on Vieques in comparison to the large neighboring island of Puerto Rico; malformed births became more frequent; and emotional problems were on the rise.

WHEN A CIVILIAN GUARD, David Sanes Rodríguez, was struck and killed in April 1999 during an "accidental firing" of 263 rounds of depleted uranium munitions by a Marine Corps pilot, the Vieques people responded with a call on the Navy to halt all bombing. In early December 1999, a women's group blocked the Navy entrance gate. Others established a protest camp at that gate to Camp Garcia, the land access to the Navy-controlled east end of the island.

Juan Figueroa, a Church of the Brethren pastor in one of the poor barrios of San Juan, urged me to ask CPT to establish a team to support the resistance efforts of the people of Vieques. Fairly quickly, CPT asked me to check out the situation to see if it fit the criteria for CPT involvement. So I visited Vieques with the support of Juan and his co-pastor wife Isabel Martinez.

A trip to the bombing zone revealed growing resistance camps—fishers, the Independence Party, Catholics, students, women, teachers, an ecumenical Protestant group, and military veterans. A Vietnam War vet had started uncovering, defusing, and flagging a field of antipersonnel mines set along the bombing zone. Vehicle mechanics repaired abandoned troop carriers to form a fleet of taxis for the scattered encampments. Gasoline from the tanks of broken-down vehicles provided fuel for this fleet. Navy personnel came at night to remove the flagged mines.

I quickly found a home in the ecumenical camp. I discovered water purification systems, solar and wind generators, a small chapel, garden plants growing, and new buildings going up in the area around the camps. This resistance community saw itself as part of the rescue and development of this devastated land so that it could be returned to the local population.

However, the US Navy saw this as a distinctly unique island, one of a kind in the world. "We will never leave," said commanding officer, Admiral Kevin Greene. Those words were quite final, and spoken by an officer of the most powerful military force the world has ever seen, they must carry a substantial amount of weight.

What can an unarmed and small group of people do in the face of that declaration? What kind of nonviolent campaign could even make a dent in the face of that overwhelming wall of "No!"? What would a campaign look like? What would be its components? Who would be involved? What steps could be possible? How would it start? How long would it take?

This US military had its war colleges, billions of dollars at its disposal, the lobby efforts of huge corporations relying primarily on weapons procurements by the US Defense Department, a bought Congress, and millions of foot soldiers under its command.

This nonviolent campaign had a few dozen fishers, a fringe political party, churches that were usually divided by political allegiances, a very poor island with seven thousand people, and some connections with peace and justice organizations. Lt. Jeff Gordon, one of the Navy officers that CPT met at a later point, helpfully pointed out that this was a David and Goliath struggle—and the Navy was David. So maybe for the nonviolent campaigners, this shouldn't have been seen as such a big hurdle!

By the time CPT came with its first delegation in March 2000, the effort was well-established. CPT would not be a prime mover but a small supportive presence. Nine delegations would only arrive sporadically over the next three years, before the US Navy pulled out. Not only did they leave the island of Vieques, but also the Puerto Rican-based Roosevelt Roads Naval Station, the largest US Navy base outside the US mainland. Part of the naval station reopened in 2017 after Hurricane Maria.

WHILE I WAS CHECKING out the struggle in February, the campaign held a silent march in San Juan, the capital of Puerto Rico. Silent and dressed in white, it was a flow of power as it took over all six lanes of the Expressway of the Americas. There had never been such a protest in Puerto Rico. I conservatively estimated that two hundred seventy thousand participants were there calling for the Navy to stop the bombing and clean up the mess.

It was surprising for locals to find Catholics and Protestants united, political parties united, veterans and peace activists on the same boat, and educated leaders and not-so well-educated workers with the same goals. Admittedly there were those who supported the continuing Navy presence in Puerto Rico. Some did so because of their jobs, while others tried to side with power, as the political climate found the US government standing with the Navy.

The first CPT delegates in March met with Navy personnel, visited the different resistance encampments in the bombing zone, and met with evangelical and Catholic leaders. They spent time with the fishers who planted the seeds of this resistance and listened to environmental folks who were trying to understand the bigger picture of the Navy's impact. The delegation met with groups from the Church of the Brethren and Mennonite churches of Puerto Rico, to encourage them to be involved in the campaign. Political officials met with the delegation and there was a press conference at the end of the visit.

Some of the young activists from the island had chosen to live in and near an abandoned tank on a hill in the bombing zone. The tank had often been a target for fighter jets and I noticed the signature holes of depleted uranium weapons. DU burns through metal as a cigarette burns through cloth. This hill was its own resistance camp that overlooked the most heavily bombed section of the zone. The activists were guinea pigs because of the toxins and radioactivity. At one point, a local activist named Cassimar tested at thirty-seven times the acceptable level of radiation. He had lesions and rashes all over his body after hunkering down inside the tank during the days a hurricane passed over.

Nilda Medina and Robert Rabin were partners who invested themselves in the coordination of this long-term struggle. They lived in a house across the road from the Camp Garcia gate and served as the energizing facilitators of the campaign. The area around that house, and across the road in front of the gate, became a fertile circle of creativity and organization for the next three years. That civilian protest encampment controlled who entered and left the Navy base. Woven ribbons tied the gate shut and tents sprouted on both sides of the entrance road, so there were always persons on watch to guard the entrance. Robert and Nilda's leadership and spirit were key to this nonviolent effort.

Saturday nights were rally events with popular musicians, speakers, and teaching/strategizing updates for the campaign. Congressional Representatives from the states were often guests at the camp and environmental leaders came to offer their support. There were tight connections with other resistance struggles confronting US bases in Korea, Italy, and Okinawa, Japan. Activists visited back and forth and learned from each other's nonviolent efforts.

News media gave prominent footage to the ongoing struggle. Hunger fasts, marches, parades, penny polls in local schools, and museum displays all built momentum for the struggle. Rallies in New York City, where there was a large Puerto Rican population, built stateside interest in, and support for, the events roiling Vieques.

CPT delegations can be cautious at first. When their flight landed and the ferry brought the second delegation to Vieques, JoAnne Lingle and I met them with a choice. "Do you want to go to the resistance camps in the bombing zone and risk probable arrest with Cliff, or go with JoAnne to the encampment at the entrance to Camp Garcia where there will likely be an opportunity to step back from a potential arrest? You have about a half hour before the boat leaves for the bombing zone so your choice has to happen fairly quickly." They all chose to go with Cliff into the bombing zone.

This step was one of a much larger process that led to the scenario described at the start of this chapter. All the people living in the bombing zone were arrested, except for a handful. With personal stashes of water, these few evaded arrest and stayed in the bombing zone to appear later when bombing restarted. Of course, their appearance again halted the bombardment, because the Navy realized that another death in the zone would further inflame and grow the resistance.

Security also arrested a large group of other resisters at the gate where Joanne had gone. That group was placed on a slow boat to the mainland, while the folks arrested in the bombing zone had Huey helicopter rides to Roosevelt Roads Naval Station on the main island. There a military judge handed down quick convictions of trespass, and the large group experienced a mad bus ride across the island to the US federal prison in Guaynabo.

Along the route, passing drivers who realized what this caravan represented joined in honking support for the prisoners. Guards escorting the prisoners in accompanying vehicles roughly stopped those supporters and threatened them with automatic weapons. At the prison after the intake process, there was a thunderous welcome for the activists when the prison population found the cause for their imprisonment. So, prison authorities soon separated these activists from the main population.

This drama in some similar fashion was to repeat itself frequently over the course of the nonviolent campaign. The arrests brought stirring news coverage which served as a recruiting tool for the effort. The Puerto Rican Bar Association offered the services of its lawyers *pro bono* for the cases of the defendants.

Sometimes those arrested were released after a short detention. If there had been an earlier arrest, the sentences of the court were often fines, jail time, or probation. The system worked hard to keep the right of a jury trial out of reach of these political prisoners. It was clear that any jury formed from the island of Puerto Rico would quickly hand down an acquittal!

The Navy's dominance in military prowess was not helpful in this setting. Their larger ships were no match for the agile fishing boats that could maneuver the shallow waters around Vieques. The fishers' knowledge of the coastal waters provided a distinct advantage as they carried new protesters out to the disputed space.

PUBLIC OPINION SWEPT BEHIND *the nonviolent campaign. The residue of war does not play well in the home country. A high percentage of Puerto Rican youth had served in war after war for the United States, and when home they did not relish another military occupation, this time of their homes.*

With the involvement of churches, including Protestant and Roman Catholic, denominational linkages to the states brought new allies to the struggle. The moral components of the resistance efforts trumped the legal efforts of the Navy. Despite Jeff Gordon's image of the Navy as David and the resistance as Goliath, the public reversed that image and threw its strong support behind the small nonviolent campaign to oust the US Navy.

Public opinion is essential in a nonviolent campaign. Without the public outcry, the activists become solitary witnesses and can more easily be crushed, as in Egypt and elsewhere across the Middle East in 2011. The Vieques campaign worked hard to maintain that visibility in the face of the dominant power of the Navy. That persistence tipped the scales of popular opinion toward the resistance.

I am sure that the security operation, when arresting hundreds of activists from the main gate and the bombing zone, was also a training exercise for the US military. How should they confront nonviolent movements? What tactics work best? My sense is that inherent in nonviolence is a bent toward justice and peace. The tools of nonviolence do not work well for authoritarianism or injustice. Maybe the days of the Arab Spring in Egypt were thrown back into dictatorship again, but the spirit of openness and justice remains in the heart of activists. And that spirit will rise again.

The visibility and news coverage at every step of this Vieques nonviolent campaign kept the activists and the events of the struggle at the forefront of televisions and newspapers. In Egypt, the torture and imprisonment were widespread. Deaths were common and no major ally came behind the Arab Spring. In Vieques, the role of the churches was key. Support from Congress brought the issue into the states on the mainland. CPT delegates from all over the US and Canada took the stories home, where they grew and gained momentum like snowballs on a hill. No international delegates spread that kind of energy from Egypt. No big institutions took the side of the protesters in Tahrir Square in Cairo.

The Muslim Brotherhood in Egypt stood as an ally but was seen by outsiders in the US and Europe as questionable. Perhaps the Independence Party outside of Puerto Rico held a similar image but other allies tipped the scales in the Vieques Campaign.

Cleanup of the bombing zone may happen, with difficulty. It has not happened yet. It seems the US military can usually avoid those responsibilities. Wars have been seen as necessary and the consequences are taken in stride as unfortunate happenstances.

The influence of money hampered the ability of the people of Vieques to shape and control the economic development of the island. Money easily manipulates people. Monied tourist companies can purchase and shape tourism for their own benefit rather than that of the island as a whole.

Perhaps a parallel effort, separate from and simultaneous with the nonviolent activist struggle, would have made the economic rescue of the island more of a possibility. Resistance groups have not traditionally done the hard work needed to shape the constructive campaigns that Gandhi and Badsha Khan saw as essential if independence was to flower. Perhaps this avenue of the struggle needs more skill, training, and creative expertise than the activist struggle. There needs to be care that the economic infrastructure of the empire is not assumed to be the path for transformation. An entirely new way of doing economics must be shaped if changes are to be sustained and meaningful.

The Zapatistas in Chiapas, Mexico probably have some of the best handles on this type of transformation. In parallel with the Zapatistas, the Abejas communities in Chenalhó Municipality worked to develop new coffee structures through organic fair trade routes to Europe and North America. Those were often based in tight Abejas nonviolent communities that stood in solidarity with the rejection of the North American Free Trade Agreement (NAFTA). When NAFTA forced three million people to leave Chiapas for the possibility of jobs in the north, the Abejas figured out a way to stay. See more in chapter 17.

Chapter 19

Into Palestine

ON JANUARY 17, 2011, I returned from a rapid round trip to the Ben Gurion Airport in Tel Aviv, Israel. I had been on my way to join the CPT group in At-Tuwani, a Palestinian community in the rural region south of Hebron, in Palestine's West Bank. One of the winter tasks was to accompany Palestinian grade school students walking to and from school. Israel would not allow a bus into their village, and Israeli settlers would frequently harass and physically attack those students when they had to walk. This was my first trip to Palestine after being turned back from entry to Israel in 1998. At that point, I was refused entry after five years of very active participation in the work of CPT in both Gaza and the West Bank.

I am one of many human rights observers and peacemakers who have been refused entry to Israel because of our work in Palestine. But this only a small slice of the massive refusal of entry to Palestinians returning to their homes from visits, school, hospital, and other trips. Palestinian rejections are part of a calculated policy to turn back the Palestinian demographic advantage over Israel. This is especially true for Palestinian residents of Jerusalem. The Israeli population is increasing more slowly than that of the Palestinians.

Expulsions and entry refusals of internationals are on the rise, as Israel and the United States are feeling fear and a loss of control over the dramatically changing political scene in the Middle East. The Right to Enter Campaign has some statistics on the numbers of Palestinians who have not been allowed to return home after trips away. Israeli refusals of CPTers trying to enter have grown from seven, in the twelve years since 1997, to eight in just the two-year period from 2010 to 2012. Of the number of their refusals, the International Solidarity Movement reported that, "you could safely say dozens." For the World Council of Churches Ecumenical Accompaniment Program in Israel, "the rate of entry has not changed." The Italian volunteer program, Operation Dove, did not respond to my emails.

As I write, the Temporary International Presence in Hebron (TIPH) has just been halted by Israel. TIPH was placed in a monitoring role in 1994 by Palestine and Israel after the massacre of twenty-nine Muslim worshipers in the Il Ibrihimi Mosque by a rightwing Israeli settler who was also a physician.

This chapter reports on one of those refusals of entry and reflects on the changing politics, in order to provide encouragement to Palestinians in their bold effort to shape a new and different future.

In the January monthly meeting of the CPT Northern Indiana regional group, Rich Meyer told me about Israeli Rabbi Arik Asherman's sendoff of Art Gish to his home after one of his stints in Palestine with CPT. Arik asked Art, "Are there poor people in your community of Athens, Ohio?" When Art responded affirmatively, Arik handed him a US one-dollar bill and requested that he share it with a street person in Athens. Arik went on to explain, "If you are on a mission of mercy, your journey will be protected."

After recounting this story, Rich then proceeded to hand me three one-dollar bills and requested that I hand one each to three of my Palestinian friends, Hani, Zeleika, and Atta, for their respective projects in Palestine. One would have thought that this would have provided adequate protection for me in my travels!

I flew on the afternoon of January 15, 2011, from the airport in Fort Wayne, Indiana, to Atlanta, Georgia. I used the security process at the airport in Fort Wayne as a time to tell the four security personnel who dealt with me that this process was an affront to the modesty of many people, and that it seemed, unfortunately, to be an exercise in response to threats instead of a proactive action to change the fear that dominates the political and public spheres in the US.

In Atlanta, I chose not to interact with folks in the waiting lounge even though I had a four-hour layover. I expected those interactions would have made their entry into Israel more difficult, as well as my own. I was intrigued to notice lots more Palestinians than I usually saw in the airports of Chicago and New York. Palestinians seemed very self-assured and relaxed as they prepared to fly back to Palestine via Israel, their only route home. Yes, travelers can fly to Amman, Jordan, then travel overland to Palestine. But travelers still must pass through Israeli security at the Allenby Bridge before being allowed into the West Bank which is Palestinian.

Upon landing in Tel Aviv, I found a short line for foreign visitors. The immigration agent asked why I was visiting, how long I planned to stay, and if I was traveling with a group. She tried to swipe my passport through the computer reader, but her computer apparently would not accept it. She asked me to go to the waiting room where there was a television, while she had someone else with a different computer try to read my passport. I suspect the computer program had flagged my name.

Shortly, a security person asked me to come with him to an office. A female agent at the desk repeated the original questions and asked where I was staying. The Golden Gate Hostel in the Old City of Jerusalem seemed not unusual. At this juncture, and with the male agent as he returned and took his place at the same desk, I shared openly that I was a volunteer with CPT and had been in Israel during the nineties.

I told the agents about the time CPTers had ridden Israeli bus #18 in Jerusalem after that bus line had been hit two times on successive weekends by Palestinian suicide bombers. That CPT action had been an effort to protest acts of violence. I didn't feel any need to tell the security agents that I had been expelled in 1998. Most of the expulsions around that time had been for only three to six years, though I had not been told if my expulsion was for any specific length of time, or even what it was for. I did comment that one of the things I appreciated about Israel was its willingness to let the truth speak for itself and not feel a need to hide the realities of the situation from outside eyes. Maybe I was trying to create a spirit that was not necessarily present in Israel.

After being asked to wait just outside the office on a chair, I was shortly escorted back to the waiting room where soccer matches were playing themselves out on the television. The others in the room, folks I recognized from the lounge in Atlanta, did not grant much eye contact. It was a longer wait this time, but soon an agent asked me to come with him to another office.

Here I greeted two female agents as well as the escort. One of them sat almost out of sight behind a movable wall while the other two sat behind the desk asking questions. They offered the expected preliminary questions and then additional requests for home phone, cell phone (I don't have one), and email addresses. I gave my phone number and an email address, but chose not to give another, the one I share with spouse Arlene, so as not to risk unwanted harassment for her.

The male agent asked who would meet me and I explained I would just join the team in Hebron on the second day before going on to the project in At-Tuwani. "Who are you meeting?" he asked. "What is the address of the apartment? What is the phone number?" I did not know the names of the CPTers who would be in Hebron, nor did I remember the address of the apartment, and I chose not to give the phone number of the Hebron team. The male agent asked, "How will you travel to Hebron? Will you go on the bus to Kiryat Arbah [the Israeli settlement on the outskirts of Hebron]?"

I detailed the step by step process of catching the Palestinian bus to Bethlehem and another bus on to the market in Hebron. Even though I didn't remember the address of the apartment I had helped clean and prepare as a team house back when the project started in 1995, I assured security that I could find it by walking there. The agent was skeptical, saying he was assigned to Hebron while in the Israeli military and knew it better than he did the airport at Ben Gurion. "Lots has changed in the intervening years," he said.

At this point, I leaned onto the table and explained with open hands, "A great deal *is* changing here in Israel/Palestine. The nonviolent movement in Palestine is making great strides. In fact, Israel is arresting and jailing the nonviolent leadership to try to halt that progress. Many countries around the world are choosing to recognize Palestinian sovereignty and the pre-1967 borders before the major incursions by Israel into the West Bank and Gaza and even East Jerusalem—all areas recognized by the international community as Palestinian territory. Even the European Union is upgrading its diplomatic status with Palestine. The boycott of Israeli products [with bar codes starting with the numbers 729 or the "Made in Israel" identification], the divestment from companies profiting because of the Israeli occupation of Palestine, and the call for sanctions against Israel are adding pressure on Israel."

The agent responded that his training was in that field, so he was familiar with all that but it wasn't going to change anything today.

By this time, I was clear that I was not going to At-Tuwani this trip. When I re-entered the waiting room, the Palestinians gave me knowing smiles, apparently as aware as I that I was on the outward-bound track. By now I had been assigned my own private security guard who was with me wherever I went.

Shortly after, security took me out to the baggage claim hall and explained that they were going to check my luggage. I asked to make a call to the US Embassy. The security guard said that could happen at a later time.

I took a bathroom break while the guard promised he would watch my back packs, which then went into the baggage claim area. I assured him I had no other luggage, and then met a person with a badge indicating he was the director of security. I was asked to sit in one of the chairs along the wall. I began to talk to my guard about the changing political scene, but the guard soon interrupted and said he wasn't allowed to talk with me.

So I got up and approached the head of security. I asked if he knew Rabbi Arik Asherman. When he seemed to indicate that he did, I told the story of the protected journey if on a mission of mercy. "Why did it not suffice here?"

"Your choice," said security.

"No it isn't; my choice would have me going on into Palestine," I responded.

Then I explained that, as director of security, he did have choices, though. Given the changing situation he could choose not to uphold unjust laws. He could be part of the changes toward justice with the Palestinians.

Two young Israeli women joined us, and I was told we would all go to another area of the terminal to examine my luggage. In this separate room, seven different people gathered over the next hour to process my two back-packs and search my body. In previous luggage checks in an earlier decade I had seen many others going through the same process, but this time I was all alone.

While the women were examining my belongings a security person took me into a separate room. I had to remove my belt, shoes, money pouch, flash drive necklace, and everything from my pockets. Security wanded me, took everything away to be x-rayed, and then did a very thorough pat down of my body. I continued telling stories of CPT.

Back in the larger room, security explained I would have to pack my small liquids and gels in a checked bag since I couldn't carry those items on the plane. I re-loaded my packs accordingly and the process allowed time to relate many more stories about CPT and the changing political scene in Palestine/Israel. After the search and repacking process was completed, the security detail departed and only two escorted me back to the waiting room.

I began again explaining the new political situation to my personal guard who told me again that I could not speak with him. A Palestinian I had seen earlier in the evening came into the room. Knowing that I would not have other opportunities to give encouragement to Palestinians on this trip, I began to talk more personally with this representative Palestinian. The guard separated us and said we couldn't talk with each other. So, I began to speak to the silent TV where a new soccer match was being played out on the screen. The Palestinian responded with smiles and nods of agree-ment as I told stories and commented on the political situation. The guard interjected with, "That's not true!" at points.

I would respond with, "But yes, it is." The dialogue continued with the new rules I had adapted. I wonder at this point what rules and games Israeli security uses in such expulsion processes?

Soon guards took my larger pack away to the plane. Then there was a small conference in the hall during which I again requested a phone call to the US Embassy. The first security person I had met after my initial contact at the immigration desk was back and told me, "Israel has decided not to allow you to enter Israel and decided not to allow a phone call. You can call the embassy when you get back to the United States because you are a US citizen. You will not be allowed to return until 2020 and then you will need a written letter from the Minister of the Interior. We will be taking you soon to the plane."

I asked to use the bathroom to wash up and change clothes. A different security person was brought to accompany me. He would not allow me to close the door, but seemed to have orders to keep his eyes on me at all times—maybe expecting a mad dash for Palestinian territory?

After this, the personal guard and a new person led me through a back elevator and hallways into the main terminal and to the exit gate. All other passengers were on board. My guards took me down the jetway and inside the door of the plane. They gave my passport to a steward explaining that he should return it to me after arrival in Atlanta. The stub to reclaim the checked backpack was in the passport, but the ticket only went as far as Atlanta. It did not include the leg of the flight to Fort Wayne. Israeli security only wanted me out of Israeli space and not in Palestinian space.

Later I wrote to a friend, describing my experience of Palestinian resilience: "Something very dramatic is happening. People that have very little apparent power are nonviolently confronting a powerful Israel, armed and supported without question by the mightiest nation the world has ever known. That small nonviolence is supported by concerned people around the world. Pressure is building on Israel and the United States as many new countries are recognizing a Palestine separate from Israel. Israel and the US are fearful and losing control of the ways they have usually used to avert unwanted change.

"Palestinians are uniting in a nonviolent campaign to end the illegal occupation of their country by Israel. That nonviolent campaign has attracted and often been led by their youth. Hundreds of those young people are going to places like South Africa to sharpen their nonviolent skills. This time they are gathering support from worldwide religious communities, unions, and dedicated peace and justice groups.

"Groups from across the political spectrum are sending relief ships and convoys into Gaza to protest the Israeli wars against Gaza and the criminal closure of the borders. Those borders are closed just because Israel and the United States did not approve the political party elected by the people of Gaza to represent them. Interestingly, the youth of Gaza have written an open appeal condemning not only the US and Israel for this closure, but also the heavy handed actions of Hamas and the Palestinian Authority in their crude attempts to maintain a united front toward the occupation.

"The tide is changing. When I return it will be Palestinian security that will have to clear me before I visit friends in Bethlehem and Hebron. Maybe this was a protected journey."

RETELLING THIS STORY REMINDS me of other passages through this terminal. After my arrest in 1997 for attempting to rebuild a Palestinian home demolished by Israeli security against the order of the Israeli Prime Minister, I spent time in Ashkelon Prison on the coast. I was in a cell with two young Israelis charged with stealing cars. On Easter Sunday I went before the judge. He ordered my keepers to allow me to return to Hebron for my belongings and to assure I was at the airport at the time my ticket was scheduled to take me home.

So on travel day, two prison guards loaded me into a prison van with metal seats and stiff wire mesh all around the back compartment. I was in leg irons, handcuffed, and with chains around my waist. I bounced all over the back on the ride to the airport. My guards did not know the way so I had to tell them through the back window of the cab how to get there.

Initially we went directly into the main terminal where I met teammates who had brought my backpack, for which I had not been allowed to return to Hebron. In the midst of us catching up with each other, my guards "came to their senses" and rushed me out of that visible location and onto the outside tarmac.

We were at the bottom of the ramp leading to the plane as passengers boarded. Two prison guards with a bearded prisoner wrapped in chains and hobbled with leg irons waited in clear view. The prison guards had never been on a plane so I urged them to come up as I boarded so they could at least see the inside. When they escorted me in, now unshackled, there was an audible gasp. I guess other riders had not expected this prisoner to be a passenger!

The trip home went well, and I had no trouble re-entering Israel after that unusual escort out of Israel. It was on a later trip, May 2000, that I spent extra time again at the airport in Tel Aviv. On my arrival I was taken to "a waiting place," this time a locked cell inside the airport. I was not allowed to contact the CPT team, though I did leave two unreturned messages at the US Embassy, citizens rights section, and my guards said they had called as well.

That cell was unique in my experience. It measured 10 feet by 12 feet. It was an apparent United Nations cell. There were fellow inmates from across the world! I remember prisoners from Russia, Pakistan, Gaza, Thailand, Moldova, Czech Republic, South Africa, and Ukraine! Notes on the walls represented at least eighteen other countries. The population changed frequently but at bedtime there were six beds for ten of us.

I guess Israel has lots of security fears. I figured out that most of these travelers were probably in the country for employment opportunities unrelated to transforming the unjust relationships between Israelis and Palestinians. I was held thirty-two hours and was the last one in the room when guards loaded me on the next flight back to Montreal and on to Chicago.

THE STRUGGLE FOR JUSTICE and peace in Palestine and Israel is the perfect arena for nonviolence. Both peoples have been the target of extreme injustice while both have also been the perpetrators of violence. The imbalance of power has been heavily tilted in favor of Israel because of its First World status and its alliance with the United States.

The United States has made Israel its largest recipient of foreign aid for decades. Israel is not poor by any standard, but aid has focused on military aid, with additional loans that become grants since Israel never has to pay back those loans.

Israel is one of a handful of nuclear powers in the world and has a diverse and strong economy. Security costs, as with the US during Vietnam or the recent escapades in West Asia, are debilitating for the rest of the economy, so Israel relies on US assistance.

The US also has granted a tiny fraction of that aid amount to Palestine and some security training for the Palestinian Authority. This may be an unsuccessful attempt to convince outsiders that the US is unbiased and deserves the role of mediator between the two parties.

A situation of injustice and violence can only be maintained with extreme control. With Israel's control of the major tools of violence, and reliance on the reliable veto by the US in United Nations settings, that control has been almost complete. Media coverage has been part of that control. The Israeli perspective has dominated the news until just recently. The Palestinian perspective has been invisible. The Israeli occupation of Palestine has been essentially unhindered by the world community.

Now that is changing with the emphasis by Palestinians on the tools of nonviolence. The Kairos document issued by faith communities in Palestine is *a call for even-handed justice for the benefit of both Israelis and Palestinians. Support has been swinging toward Palestine since the European Union and even the United States often vote or act in directions that Israel would not have them do. The recognition of Palestine by United Nations bodies and the US-brokered treaty with Iran over nuclear disarmament are cases in point. The US involvement in the Iran treaty has now been rolled back by the Donald Trump administration.*

The Boycott/Divestment/Sanctions (BDS) Campaign has been instrumental in those changes. The international boycott of companies that uphold the occupation, divestment from Israeli companies located in the West Bank on Palestinian land, and sanctions against Israel for its ongoing illegal occupation of Palestine are indicators of a deteriorating control by Israel.

Clearly international support is key to this nonviolent movement. Now larger numbers of people and nations are clearly recognizing the injustice of the occupation and that is making the difference. A minority cannot continue the ways of violence when their deeds become visible and global political and economic pressures are brought to bear against the oppression inherent in the Israeli occupation of Palestine.

Will the injustices continue being visible? Will that pressure continue until Palestine has control over its own economy, politics, and security? Will earlier injustices be compensated by Israel so that Palestine has an opportunity to rebuild its future?

Chapter 20

Depleted Uranium Campaign in Tennessee

In the spring of 2005, there was a Christian Peacemaker Team on the ground in Baghdad, Iraq. Part of the regular long-term team planning was to lay out an action agenda for the coming year. The agenda sought to reduce the violence in the region where the team was based. It was also to work in conjunction with the local groups that had invited CPT to Iraq, and who were key in shaping a local action plan.

One item the team selected for the agenda that year was a focus on ending the use of depleted uranium (DU) weapons. Choosing this focus was a recognition that the conflict in Iraq was intimately tied to business back in North America, a place most of the team members at that time called home.

An important step in the process of building a nonviolent campaign is to nurture times of brainstorming. Brainstorming is a process with a space to allow the mind and spirit to flow freely. The mind can then make serendipitous connections that suggest ways to move forward or build momentum in a campaign. It is a creative space where no suggestion is rejected, and all ideas are recorded. That list becomes the stockpile from which pieces are drawn to build the structure of the campaign. Later in the campaign, planners may return to the stockpile for ideas that more clearly fit in terms of timing and strategy. Please see Appendix D for an unorganized list of brainstorming ideas that came out of different sessions early on in our DU campaign.

WHEN A DEPLETED URANIUM weapon strikes a hard surface, the DU aerosolizes into nanoparticles that are scattered into the air and soil. Researcher Rosalie Bertell found that the pyrophoric, flammable nature of DU leads to 20–70% of the uranium becoming aerosolized in the explosion of a shell.

Those ceramic nanoparticles of low-level radioactive DU can easily enter the body. Because of its density, it often lodges in and around internal organs, especially the lungs. There, the alpha particles can wreak havoc with genes, the immune system, and regular body functions. Because it is ceramic, it will not dissolve easily to be flushed from the body, as the usual line of bodily defense does with radioactive substances.

In 2003, John Little, at the Harvard School of Public Health, uncovered the "bystander effect." Cells that have not encountered radioactive particles, but are near those that have been exposed, can also be changed or damaged, just as the cell that did encounter the radioactivity.

What would it take to organize an effort to end depleted uranium weapons? There already is a global effort to stop nuclear weapons. It has led to major cuts in the stockpiles of United States and Soviet Union nuclear warheads and applicator tools. Presently, those agreements have been between the United States and Russia, the states with the largest nuclear stockpiles. Depleted uranium munitions have some of the same hazards as nuclear weapons, but they are becoming ubiquitous around the globe with few restrictions.

In 2015, the world saw many of the nuclear weapons nations fashion an agreement with Iran to stay its development of nuclear weapons capability. Yet this impetus is not universal in its application, as Israel and North Korea are still wild cards outside any global nuclear restrictions.

WHEN CPT ARRIVED IN Iraq the fall of 2002, one of the early activities was to visit southern Iraq near Basrah. This was the area that had suffered the brunt of the US assault in 1991, in response to the Iraqi invasion of Kuwait in August 1990. Much of Iraq's military capability was crushed by the overwhelming air and ground pressure from A-10 Warthogs and Abrams tanks armed with depleted uranium munitions.

Major Doug Rokke had put together the protection plan for US military personnel. It was to protect them from the chemical and radioactive threats of the depleted uranium munitions that were to be used during that US assault. As it turned out, the officers never passed on the protection plan to the soldiers. Doug was told the reason: ground troops would never have fought if they had seen the dangers to them from their own weapons.

After the victory, Doug was asked to put together a cleanup crew of three hundred for the US equipment that had been hit by friendly fire DU weapons. He told a CPT group that half of the crew was either dead or had cancer by the time we visited him in his home in 2006. This was despite using recommended protective gear and precautionary action that was to have prevented problems.

Depleted uranium munitions have some distinct advantages on the battlefield. They are denser than lead, so they carry about two miles further than traditional shells; they can pierce the armor on tanks; they can take out deep underground bunkers; and they can even blast through sand hills to destroy enemy tanks on the other side. As a waste product from the nuclear enrichment process, DU is also relatively inexpensive.

However, DU has some disadvantages to the human body. It is slightly radioactive and has heavy metal chemical toxicity. Alexandra Miller and David McClain, working for the Armed Forces Radiobiology Research Institute, found that depleted uranium has six to eight times the expected negative impact on the human body when the nuclear and chemical hazards are considered in combination (The Guardian, April 17, 2003). DU also has a half-life of four and a half billion years, so that negative impact will hang around for a while.

CPT visited three children's hospitals in the Iraqi cities of Basrah, Baghdad, and Mosul in 2003. In all three, a scourge of very unusual births had been occurring. Babies were born without limbs, one eye, no brain, and organs outside their bodies. Their parents had been in the military or lived in the region that received heavy US military bombardment in 1991. There were also high rates of cancers and leukemias. These rates of birth defects and cancers started to increase gradually three to five years after the 1991 military assault on Iraq by the US. Then the graphs spiked radically upward in the ensuing years.

Just before the 2003 US invasion of Iraq (during which hundreds of tons of DU weapons were again used) CPT was taking visiting delegations to hear the reports of Iraqi Dr. Alim Yacoub. He had done the most in-depth recording and study of these DU-related health aberrations in Iraq. Dr. Yacoub was employed by the United Nations World Health Organization (WHO) at their office in Baghdad. Soon he was telling us, "We may not speak about these DU-related issues anymore." He indicated that there were microphones in the ceiling of the room in which we met, and he had been silenced on these issues. Who would not want the scientific community to discover what might be behind these health tragedies? Who would benefit from this dearth of knowledge? Who would have the power to shut down the voice of the WHO?

CPT made arrangements to meet with him outside the WHO office. But he, along with his teenage daughter and son, died in a suspicious automobile accident before we could meet.

How does a group build a nonviolent campaign, this one focused on ending DU weapons? First, pay attention to the news. On returning to the states, CPTers saw an article about a new military contract for DU weapons. It was clear that three companies were involved. Aerojet Ordnance in Jonesborough, Tennessee, manufactured the penetrator core of the DU shell. Radford Arsenal in Virginia provided the propulsion feature of the shell. Those components were assembled in Rocket City, West Virginia, by the ATK Tactical Systems. Keeping a broad base of employment in different congressional communities helped the industry to build support for such a contract.

CPT visited all three sites in March 2006. It became clear that the Jonesborough site was the key to the operation. If the campaign goal was to stop DU production, it only needed to stop the penetrator core stage. So, Tennessee became the focus.

CPT had a forty-five-minute March meeting in the entryway of the plant with Pepper McCary, head of the health, environmental, and safety efforts of Aerojet Ordnance. Return visits to Aerojet Ordnance plant made it clear that was to be the last time any plant official would be allowed to meet with CPT during the campaign. Press conferences across the road from the plant with invitations for the officers of the plant to bring their own data and perspectives were rejected. It appeared they felt the less visibility the plant experienced the better chance they had of weathering this campaign.

A CPT delegation in May 2007 released helium balloons from the road in front of the Aerojet Ordnance plant. These airborne communication tools informed the recipients that in the event of an accident at Aerojet they would be on the receiving end of any airborne dangers as well.

Linda Modica in Tennessee became the local go-to woman. She was past president of the local Sierra Club. She connected CPT to local churches and assisted with contacts in the academic communities. In September, there was a meeting of interest in a nearby community that brought other individuals and groups into the struggle. Former workers at Aerojet and neighbors of the plant rallied around the effort. Visits to staff at the Veterans Administration Hospital in a neighboring city and VA hospitals in other areas of the country began to uncover data: US veterans who had been in Iraq and Afghanistan were experiencing some of the same health problems faced by Iraqis.

Around this time, in pursuit of Osama Bin Laden, the US was dropping DU bunker buster bombs into the mountains of Tora Bora, Afghanistan. So Afghanistan also became a focus of our nonviolence campaign.

During this delegation, Doug Rokke agreed to be one of the resource persons for a national conference on Depleted Uranium at East Tennessee State University on May 19, 2007. Other newcomers to CPT on the panel were Cathy Garger, a writer on DU issues, and Mohammad Daud Miraki, PhD in Public Policy and author of Afghanistan after Democracy.

Miraki's book has detailed data and graphic pictures of birth defects and cancers in his country, similar to what CPT had found in Iraq. He worked for Chicago State University, but was fired from his position after speaking out against the US attack on his country.

That conference provided publicity to this community/CPT campaign and began as well to uncover the resistance from vested interests. Linda Modica, Major Doug Rokke, Cathy Garger, Dr. Mohammad Daud Miraki, and I all began to attract the interest of retired Air Force person Roger Helbig. Roger would harass us individually, trying to provoke us. He would also email and call colleagues of ours, and news reporters, to discredit us and our work.

I tried to talk directly with Roger to learn what experiences brought him to a different understanding from that which I held about DU. He refused to speak about it. He later declined to be a resource person for a delegation I was building.

A provocateur is at times inserted into an action to incite actors to respond to the provocateur rather than to the issue at hand. We need to stay focused on stopping DU munitions. Provocateurs can also be used to penetrate the leadership of a campaign and lead a nonviolent campaign into acts of violence that would stain and weaken the image of the effort.

As he spoke out against depleted uranium weapons, Doug referred to his experience in Iraq during the first Gulf War. Opponents pointed out that there was no record of his having ever served! Doug discovered that all his records had disappeared from the veterans files maintained in St Louis! This was in spite of his commendations from Commanding General Norman Schwarzkopf for his time of service in Iraq and corroboration from those with whom he served during those years.

BUILDING ALLIANCES IN A campaign often leads to unexpected partners. One of our local advisors encouraged CPT to connect with the president of the Rolling Thunder Motorcycle Brigade. This is the group that provides the motorcycle escort for returning military personnel. When meeting with a CPT delegation, we asked the Rolling Thunder president to share about his experiences in Vietnam with Agent Orange. Some of his buddies had died or were struggling with the aftereffects of that toxic herbicide. He immediately saw the parallels with DU poisoning in Iraq and Afghanistan. His brigade was leaving shortly for DC where the national commander would meet with President George W. Bush. He suggested that he would urge the commander to speak about DU issues with the president if we would go to local VFW posts to share the same. We would work from both ends of the power spectrum to bring change!

Early on, the campaign learned that other communities had already dealt with problems from the production of depleted uranium munitions. The National Lead plant in Colonie, NY, was closed because DU was found both upwind and downwind from the operations. The Starmet Corporation in Concord, MA, was terminated because of a contaminated drinking water aquifer and plumes of leukemia cases downwind from the plant. Jefferson Proving Ground in Indiana closed because the seventy tons of DU tested on these grounds could not be cleaned up. It became a hunting range. Jefferson Proving Ground would carry greater DU toxicity because of exploded ordnance than the production sites. These DU facilities were closed down successfully. It can be done.

The DU campaign in January 2007, carried out an informal health survey of every home within a half mile of the Aerojet production facility. There were many unusual cancers, headaches, and strange health concerns. There were sightings of huge bubbles escaping from the Aerojet stacks, once settling onto a ball diamond with young players, and another time floating off into the sky. The survey was an attempt to encourage the county health department to carry out a more exacting epidemiological study that could find the truth about dangers to the community from Aerojet operations. That study has not yet taken place.

I visited a Sunday School class at one church where our CPT delegation had lodged. There, members queried me about my activities with the campaign. When I explained the potential dangers that could impact the surrounding neighborhood from regular operation or accidents at Aerojet, one woman exclaimed to her husband, "Honey, you remember our dog died of cancer." Another class member commented about her cat's death from cancer. Then, a third in a class of only eight members mentioned a similar concern about his pet. Pets spending regular time in the grass would be the first to have contact with residue from airborne contamination. This Sunday School class interchange inspired visits to local veterinary clinics and questions to Cornell University, but these leads did not uncover any research or data helpful for the campaign.

Next, the local community, under the direction of Linda Modica, acquired the services of researcher Michael Ketterer from Arizona State University. Ketterer is a chemist with expertise in the movement of radioactivity through the environment. Using two spectrometers to confirm accuracy, his study crews took samples from Little Limestone Creek near the Aerojet plant and from the Nolichucky River flowing by the Nuclear Fuel Services (NFS) plant in Erwin. NFS downblends weapons grade uranium for use by the Navy and is a sister operation to Aerojet. There were points of major contamination near the NFS facility, and sufficient information to pique Ketterer's interest in a further study focused more on the land near Aerojet Ordnance.

For the second study, the team collected data from within one mile of the plant. Samples of earth were collected around the Aerojet perimeter and from the downspouts of nearby homes; water and sediment samples were taken from Little Limestone Creek; attic dust was sampled from Aerojet neighbors' homes: and samples were collected from wells in the area. These comprised the evidence gathered in the research data.

A second press conference on July 15, 2013, was sparked by the study, as Ketterer came back with the report. It clearly documented that depleted uranium had been released from the Aerojet plant contaminating the surrounding community. Yet things did not change. Jobs are very important at a time when the economy is struggling. The Chamber of Commerce was chaired by the president of Aerojet. In our surveys of the community, households with workers at the plant would usually choose not to participate. During one rally at the plant entrance, CPT was handing out leaflets to passing cars. One man pulled over on his way to work in the plant and engaged the CPTers in conversation. When we questioned the wisdom of this very visible meeting with us right across the road from the plant, he assured us that the plant wouldn't care that he was talking to us. Then he received a call on his cell phone that indicated otherwise, and he left immediately for work!

A problem with a campaign against depleted uranium weapons is that cancers don't carry a label which indicates the cause of the cancer. Pollution does carry an identifying label when studied with a mass spectrometer, but the common person does not have that device hanging on her or his tool rack. It is easy for company spokespersons to counter these community cancer concerns with threats of job losses. These jobs thus become a more urgent and real concern to people than the invisible threat.

In February 2012, the wife of one of the directors at Aerojet Ordnance called me twice. She explained that she and her daughter had serious health issues originating when her husband took his position at Aerojet and they moved into a new home downwind from the facility. Her daughter was born shortly after and within two years both faced major health complications. She expanded this statement by saying she had skin and oral cancers, early onset arthritis, undifferentiated lupus, lymphoma, skin rashes, headaches, and four very rare auto-immune disorders. Her daughter had very rare genetic mutations.

At one point the family moved away and many of the maladies cleared up. When they moved back her health problems returned with a vengeance. At the time of her calls, this woman was seeing nine different doctors, had been hospitalized four times the previous month, and was spending about $6000 per month on medications.

Her health and that of her daughter seemed directly related to her husband's work. He would come home from the plant late after not showering even though he had warned her during one visit at the plant to not cross a warning tape to use a bathroom. He had told her, "I'll never lose my job because it can never be cleaned up."

She concluded her conversation by asking to join the campaign to stop DU weapons. Could she do CPT training and go on a delegation?

How does CPT incorporate this interest without endangering her? Always there are questions of security in peacemaking. Usually they focus on the peacemakers themselves, but in this case they involve another person who asks to join the struggle. Clearly, the risks need to be made clear to the volunteer, and the volunteer must have time to make an informed decision.

Long before CPT reached this stage in the campaign the scientific community was clear about the dangers of depleted uranium. Even as early as the seventies, the military had warned of the dangers. But as with Agent Orange during Vietnam, the costs and ramifications of publicly admitting the hazards of DU would be prohibitive. It is easier to cover up the problems. To remove the contaminated soils from Iraq would be nearly impossible.

In 2001, the US Navy discontinued use of DU munitions and switched to tungsten. In 2005, the European Parliament called for a ban and moratorium on DU use by their militaries. The Parliament even recommended that no European Union (EU) troops be deployed to DU-contaminated zones. DU weapons had been used by the US and its allies in Bosnia, and then again in Serbia, Kosovo, and Montenegro. Site contamination led to calls for cleanup, and after several years serious health problems surfaced similar to those in Iraq from the 1991 war.

Though the findings by Rosalie Bertell and John Little mentioned at the beginning of this chapter were much later than the original warnings from military researchers in the seventies, those findings did confirm the concerns from the military researchers. With the wars of this new century and sale of DU weapons to dozens of other countries, the problems of DU are spreading. The US continues to use these efficient weapons, and they efficiently destroy the health of those who use them, as well as the health of intended and unintended targets of their horror.

The campaign is not completed. DU munitions are still being produced and sold around the world. What further steps should the next generation pursue?

DU production sites are not as dangerous to one's health as DU conflict zones. Aerosolized DU is much more present on battlefields. But there, health tests are more problematic. Surely the county health department near Aerojet should do an epidemiological study. But the US military should also do extensive testing of exposed US military personnel. Those tests may uncover an Agent Orange-like quagmire. But if we as a country are to be responsible, we must do the environmental cleanup work. And where it is still possible, we must do the health mitigation for any of those we have exposed to the dangers of DU radioactivity and toxicity.

Efforts need to be put into job development for those who will lose jobs when plants like Aerojet close or transform. By no longer allowing military corporations to set government policy or determine the tools to resolve conflicts, we will build stronger economies. Schools at all levels need to recognize that conflicts are resolved for the benefit of the world when nonviolent tools are employed. As CPT discovered in West Virginia, Craig Etchison became the director of the college peace program because he had been a combat soldier in Vietnam and recognized the futility of violence.

Corporations have a charter granted by local communities. Once they compromise that charter by bringing harm to a community, or neglecting to contribute any longer to that community, their charter should become revocable. Some serious nonviolent effort can be focused on this issue.

The cost of a machine or process needs to include the effort and expense that will be involved in cleaning up the mess that machine or process leaves behind. Increased cost may push it into a cost prohibitive zone and it will never be used. Such should have been the case with DU munitions. This is also true with nuclear weapons—their manufacture, testing, and storage. Our society has often abandoned dangerous waste, with later cleanup and cost covered by society rather than by the polluter itself. In a world with limits and cascading consequences, nonviolent movements should tackle this problem head on.

This campaign is not completed. I have extensive material to help move this nonviolent effort forward to completion! I invite the reader and other interested parties to carry this transformation campaign to a successful conclusion.

Chapter 21

Neither al Qaeda nor Empire

REVOLUTION USUALLY STARTS WHEN rebels pick up weapons, and the counter-revolution usually responds by picking up larger, more effective weapons. In the winter of 2011, the world observed a transformed process in the Arab Spring. In Tunisia and Egypt, revolutionaries and their adversaries paved new roads toward change. The mainly youthful protesters chose not to use the weapons controlled by those in power, and those in power recognized that their very powerful weapons would not be effective to stop the uprisings. Both the Al Qaeda option and the Empire option were rejected as worthless tools of change or stopping change.

This is a different brain pattern from how the world has usually operated. War is done with the tools of violence such as automatic weapons, tanks, fighter jets, drones, and bombs. Revolution or insurrection takes place with automatic weapons, improvised explosive devices (IEDs), suicide bombers, drones, and mortars.

It is not that those tools work effectively for any party. If they did the United States would have easily won the wars in Iraq and Afghanistan. Fighting against essentially third world military forces or weaker, it would have been like a Super Bowl football champion taking on the second-string team of the small local high school. Yet the mightiest fighting force the world has ever seen has lost both wars. The tools of violence do not work. In fact, both the Empire and the resistance have been losers in Iraq and Afghanistan. The tools of Empire do destroy everything.

Libya was an exception in this Arab Spring. There, both sides were using the obsolete tools and miring down in loss or blowback. Yemen, Bahrain, Algeria, Morocco, Jordan, Palestine, Syria, and Iraq are among other countries that were experiencing the same nonviolent spring we observed in Tunisia and Egypt. Even an Israeli general is clear: "If Palestinians choose the route of the Egyptian revolutionaries, we have nothing to stop them." The hard work of developing the constructive program still lies ahead, but it is much easier to build on the emotions left in the wake of nonviolence than on the emotions left in the wake of violence.

The people of both Iraq and Afghanistan have also been the losers. The Empire has pumped in its billions and trillions of dollars. One quality of life marker is life expectancy at birth. In that category Afghanistan is 222nd in the world with only two countries below it. Iraq, which only decades ago had one of the best education and health care systems in the Middle East, is now ranked on the CIA life expectancy scale at 117th, just above Gaza. As occupier, the United States is responsible for the well-being of those populations. On the same ranking, the United States is about 43rd, eleven ranks below Puerto Rico!

The losses in the wars are not the fault of US soldiers. They have fought bravely but have borne the brunt of the costs in our country. Over the past decades, veterans have brought home from the wars post-traumatic stress and other impacts from the conflicts. More active duty US military personnel die from suicide than die in combat, and one quarter of the homeless are veterans.

The United States allocates over fifty percent of its discretionary federal tax budget dollars on war-related expenditures, about $700 billion dollars for present budget years. But war-related expenditures include more than just the billions for the so-called defense department budget. That number is nearly half of what the entire world spends on war each year. If war could stop terror, end injustice, eliminate weapons of mass destruction, or end violence, the job would be done already! But in reality each of those problems is growing dramatically.

War does not work!

A CAVEAT HERE: WAR *does* work for corporations. They are making some of the highest quarterly profits in their history. The war corporations are at their peak. It doesn't matter which administration is in office, those corporations are winners on the fields of battle. Their CEOs are not risking their lives on the fields of battle. No, their only risk is whether they will make 25% or 100% or more on their investments, whether they will have a no-bid contract with the federal government, or have to compete with other corporations at the money troughs of war.

The dramatically new choices of tools in Tunisia and Egypt are really not new. The world has watched this nonviolent drama before. In the nonviolent Gandhian colonial uprising against Great Britain, it was an upstart colony India against the mighty British Empire. India gained its independence. Who would have imagined the fall of the Berlin Wall in 1989 and the ensuing nonviolent changes across Eastern Europe? Or the ending of apartheid and the rise to the presidency of Nelson Mandela, a prisoner of nearly thirty years in South Africa? The nonviolent tools of Martin Luther King Jr. and the Civil Rights movement in the United States provided awareness and models for these more recent actions of change.

Or which of you have seared on your brain the image of the lone student standing before the line of tanks in Tiananmen Square in China? "Sure," you say, "but who won that day?"

Yes, the tanks drove out the students that day, but who really won the battle for the hearts and minds of the people that day? It was not the tanks. The tools of listening, crossing barriers that get built between people, truth, unarmed courage, accompaniment of threatened people, persistent protest in the face of injustice, and faith-based visioning will consistently overcome the weapons of violence, usually in the short run and always in the long run.

The tools of violence are the tools of a minority that does not have justice or the people on its side. If a principle or idea is valid, it will rally its own support. It does not require a gun, a suicide bomb, or nuclear weapon to make its case. Truth campaigns for itself, maintains moral principles and resolves its own issues in the transparency of accurate news and open political processes.

Why don't ideologies or economies compete by attracting allies instead of trying to destroy the other? Are they so insecure in their own position that they need to tip the scales in other ways to compete? I would submit that any goal which requires me to kill, torture, diss, or otherwise waste another person to reach that goal is probably not what it appears to be. Some government or other agency is trying to slip something by me. It will not be worth my time or loss of values to work for that goal.

A website, www.worldgame.org, displays how the monies the nations of the world spend on war each year could be used to easily resolve the problems facing our world. Many of those problems accentuate the issues that lead to war. Lack of education, contaminated water, nuclear weapons, hunger, displaced populations, acid rain, lack of shelter, Third World debt, ozone depletion, soil erosion, global warming, finding safe renewable energy, health care and AIDS control, landmines, deforestation, and reaching stabilized populations could all be dealt with by using only one third of what the world spends yearly on war and doing that over several decades.

Clearly, empires fall. It is an historical given. But they do so more quickly when they spend most of their economics and creative energy on dead-end production. M-16s don't build houses, teach students, or plant gardens. A hoe feeds a student, who becomes a teacher, who educates a building contractor.

Additionally, empires pay for war after the fact. Countries always owe for past wars, and try to pay for present wars by borrowing on the future. In contrast, Social Security and Medicare in theory pay ahead for retirement and future health care. That plan is compromised when empires borrow from that strong reserve to pay for wars as we have done in the United States.

Nonviolence does not require massive investment. If the United States did not use half of its discretionary budget to feed war, the war corporations would not have the money to pay lobbyists and lawyers to control the decisions of Congress and the Supreme Court for the corporations' benefit. If put to a popular vote in the US, Iraq, or Afghanistan, those wars of occupation would end. Tax monies should be used to improve the resilient strength of societies.

Chapter 22

Congolese Retaking the Initiative

IN DECEMBER 2008, CPT sent a team of four to the Democratic Republic of the Congo (DRC) to test the possibility of having a permanent project in that volatile region. This team was preceded by two previous CPT learning delegations, which led to an invitation from the Martin Luther King (MLK) Groupe to place an exploratory CPT team in Goma, in the eastern DRC.

As a member of this team, I felt that I was heading into one of the most difficult situations I had faced in all my twenty years of work with CPT. The genocide of Tutsi people in neighboring Rwanda by the Hutu militias and supportive population in 1993 led to the massacre of nearly one million people in just a few months.

The response of Tutsi fighters from Uganda drove the Hutu population into eastern DRC, where there were already huge displacement camps of Tutsis who had fled the earlier fighting. There the violence continued, aided by Congolese troops and more militia groups.

When we arrived, there were nine different fighting groups. Many controlled very lucrative mines that provided abundant funding to purchase weapons and kill with abandon. Rape had become a tool of war that devastated village and societal structures. Estimates were that nearly seven million people had been killed in the DRC during the years since the genocide in Rwanda. It was the most violent conflict in the world since WWII. Vast UN refugee camps covered wasted areas outside and inside the zones of conflict. Towns and cities cowered and fled as fighting lines ebbed and flowed across this breadbasket of eastern Congo.

The DRC is a land rich in diamonds, cobalt for batteries, copper, gold, coltan for computers and cell phones, lumber, water, and oil. The DRC people are among the poorest of the world. The major countries and corporations of the world have their selfish fingers in the wealth of the DRC. They were the invisible forces behind the terrible fighting that had further destroyed this land, after being sacked by Belgian colonialism and the selfish aggrandizement of dictator Mobutu Sese Seko, who had channeled the country's wealth to himself and western countries.

As we prepared to depart from home in early December, the border with Rwanda through which we would enter the DRC was closed. A rebel Tutsi militia group with strong Rwandan support had been sweeping down eastern DRC toward Goma, taking towns and DRC military bases at will. Those militia fighters had stopped on the north edge of Goma, but it was clear they could take the city at the time of their choosing, even with United Nations troops ensconced in the city.

We got in without incident as the border opened, but I could only expect despair and disaster, with little space for the tools of nonviolence to make any difference. The Martin Luther King Groupe met the CPTers at the small border crossing with motor bikes. CPT was a strong group, with years of nonviolence experience in Mexico, Iraq, Palestine, Haiti, Colombia, and Native struggles in North America. One of our team members was fluent in Swahili after about thirty years of work in Somalia and Tanzania. We faced a formidable task. Fortunately, the work was not ours to do.

The MLK Groupe introduced CPT to some of the major civil society actors in the DRC. There was an amazing flurry of resistance to the violence and, at the same time, bold attempts to begin to rebuild the devastated society.

There was a gun buyback program that offered a bicycle in exchange for the gun when it started in Bukavu in the southeast of the Congo. Now the program is offering $100 for the turning in of any gun. The buyback program is centered in Kinshasa, the capital of the country. It is a creative effort to curtail the violence, and it provides individual families with the resources to rebuild society.

In 1998, colleagues of Pastor Luc Kuye approached him to lead the dialog process between the various fighting groups at that time. He declined, explaining that he was just a pastor, and that he didn't do politics. They encouraged and pressured him until he agreed to lead the task. That dialog process worked well.

After this they came to him again. This time it was to ask him to lead the interim government. As one might imagine, he turned it down flat, with similar reasons for his decision. They asked again until he agreed. He did an outstanding job.

Then, there were peace talks in Pretoria, South Africa, between the various rebel groups and the government. They came again to Pastor Luc Kuye. Someday it will be a Hollywood movie: imagine the tension, the drama, the high stakes politics. It was clear as the players sat around the table that the rebels had decided not to sign. Kuye started the paper around the table so that it would reach the rebel party last. They signed!

But who would go to ensure that the rebel leaders, safely living in Europe, would call off their fighters? Again, it was Kuye. Yet even if they agreed to repatriate to Rwanda, what would ensure there wouldn't be another genocide, this time against the returning Hutus and their families? So, Pastor Luc Kuye went to the Council of Churches in Rwanda to ready welcoming spaces for the Hutus.

Well, the reader will understand it wasn't just Pastor Luc Kuye. Civil society as a whole was intimately involved in the step-by-step struggle to lay down a foundation for a different future from that which stared at the country through the barrels of weapons used by the fighting factions. Every single aspect of society to this point had been controlled by those with guns. Now something new was occurring. The pastor wasn't alone in this process. He represented a larger group of religious and emerging civic leaders, a part of civil society, who decided they needed to risk shaping a new future.

Through the MLK Groupe, CPT met an amazing woman on the west shore of Lake Kivu. Maseeka lived in a small village. That village was bordered by the jungle where fighting groups found refuge. One time, a rebel militia entered the village, killing and burning. The rebels broke into Maseeka's home and killed her husband in front of her. More than a dozen of them proceeded to gang rape her and her two teenage daughters.

Maseeka was torn apart physically. She wanted to die. Someone from Synergie des Femmes, a local women's support group, found her and took her to a hospital where doctors started to put her back together physically. She was taken to a safe house where she got counseling to begin the long journey of psychological healing. She also received economic skill training so that family and village, which were likely to reject her, would instead see in her a potential engine of development for their impoverished communities.

Her daughters had babies from the rapes and asked their mother if she would care for the children. Amnesty International provided funding for the daughters to go on to school, one as a physician and the other as a social worker. Maseeka agreed to care for the babies; soon she was caring for over a dozen rape babies. Women heard about Maseeka and came to her for help. She became a stalwart figure in Synergie des Femmes.

As an advocate for women's rights, a fighter against impunity for rapists, and a person with a different vision of the future driving her forward, she crossed battle lines that few others dared to cross. She would have made the perfect CPTer in the war zones of the world. Here she was just that, but under a different name, in the most difficult war zone of the world.

Never have I seen such boldness in taking back the initiative from the actors of violence in the zones of war. Maseeka and Luc Kuye and their colleagues have taken nonviolence to a highly advanced level. They understand the necessity of confronting violence, but they also comprehend that there will never be a different future unless they themselves begin to build it on the rubble of the old. It appeared as though they had the angels of Gandhi and Badshah Khan hanging on their shoulders whispering about the constructive program!

After three months, CPT decided not to place a permanent team in the DRC. Had we stayed, our primary task would have been to just offer encouragement and support to a civil society that was already embodying peace.

Epilogue

RESURRECTION POWER IS THE renewable energy of nonviolent peacemaking. Nonviolence depends on the tools we each carry in our own hands, hearts, and minds. Nonviolence depends upon courage, creativity, and imagination undergirded with a deep spirituality. Resurrection nonviolence can be understood as the resulting compost from plowsharing the tools of violence and injustice. Using nonviolence to resolve our differences and problems doesn't break the bank or destroy our world.

So, here are some plowsharing observations that have come from my work with Christian Peacemaker Teams: 1) War does not work; 2) A nonviolent alternative stares us in the face; 3) War has been the basis for the massive transfer of public wealth and value to corporate wealth; 4) The tax monies and investments used for war could be used instead to solve the big problems looming over our world; 5) Nonviolence is democratic and builds justice for all the world; 6) Today we are observing the end of war.

What I have experienced in the dramas of Christian Peacemaker Teams is more than hope. In situation after situation the tools of war have crumbled before the committed, persistent plowsharing of nonviolent actors. The powers of empire and violent resistance want us to think that our peacemaking efforts are useless, and we should not even make any attempt at change. The reality is that those power players do not hold the strong cards. We, as committed nonviolent activists, do hold the strong cards.

Miracle plays on our team. So, hook up your plow to any renewable, spiritually undergirded energy source, and begin turning the compost from wartime residue into the rich soil of our future!

Appendix A:
General Tools of Nonviolence

1. Engage in nonviolence trainings.

2. Fast to listen and gain clarity of thoughts.

3. Develop strategic campaigns to retake the initiative from actors of violence.

4. Provide attentive accompaniment.

5. Document human rights violations.

6. Tell the stories of peace and justice in voice, pictures, written words, and actions.

7. Be willing to cross artificial barriers.

8. Be open to risk.

9. Maintain an undergirding spirituality.

10. Engage in pilgrimage as a movement toward a goal.

11. Break down stereotypes.

12. Personalize the "other."

Appendix B:
Specific Tools of Nonviolence, Personal List

To practice nonviolence, a practitioner must know that there are a variety of tools available, and that it is possible to develop new tools no one has ever used before. Nonviolence is grounded in creativity and imagination. Some tools are frequently used by a broad spectrum of society; others are quite unusual and discovered only because of an uncommon juxtaposition of events and ideas, or crises and interactions of people.

The following list is my personal list, not exhaustive, and not in any chronological order. I offer it as a stimulus for others to think back over their own lives and discover they are creative nonviolent activists! When we learn that we are so well supplied with tools it will be much easier to lay aside tools of violence that do not work and pick up more effective community peacebuilding tools. Here is the list!

1. Along with others, I picked up a sledgehammer and chisel to open the gates of Hebron University, which was sealed by the Israeli occupation for four years. 1995.

2. With other CPTers, I joined Abejas women, with children on their backs, to pass out exit visas to soldiers staffing the Majomut Mexican Military base in Chenalhó, Chiapas, Mexico. We were inviting them to go home so the displaced indigenous families could return to their homes. Holy Week, November 2001.

3. I traveled alone into the campo near Remedios and Segovia to leverage an opening for local folks displaced in this region of Antioquia, Colombia, amid paramilitary and military forces. March 2001.

4. I led over a half dozen delegations of CPTers into Vieques, Puerto Rico, where a broad resistance movement was planting encampments inside the bombing zone, an act among many that eventually led to the shutting down of that bombing zone. 2000–2002.

5. As CPT, we joined nonviolent Lakota warriors as they set up a protest encampment on La Framboise Island, Pierre, South Dakota, to resist a state government land grab. 1999.

6. Our family developed an organic market garden, an island in a sea of conventional farms. 1983–2020.

7. Since 2003, we have followed the simple practice of giving away all our produce on the final day of market each year, as a protest against accumulative capitalism and a confession of our own complicity. 2003–2019.

8. As a family we have consistently kept our yearly income below the taxable level as a protest of taxes being used for war purposes and an act of downward mobility and sustainability in a world of injustice and unsustainable living. 1971–2020.

9. I was a member of the first CPT team which was sent to the Gaza Strip. We accompanied families in the refugee camps to provide some level of protection by opening the eyes of the world to the brutal Israeli occupation. Summer 1993.

10. I joined Palestinian Grandpa Jabber and his eight-year-old granddaughter, who were sitting on the blade of the bulldozer that had come to bulldoze his home, while teammate Anne Montgomery was documenting this with her camera. That joint resistance prevented the Israeli military from destroying their home. 1997.

11. Our CPT delegation issued a ban and bar letter to the commanding officer at Roosevelt Roads Naval Base, directing him to discontinue any further use of the Vieques bombing zone. 2000.

12. With about fifty others who were part of the Iraq Peace Team, I lived in Baghdad during the "Shock and Awe" bombing campaign of the United States and its allies. This presence was a protest of that assault. March 2003.

13. As CPT, we set up tents at the Al Wathba Water Treatment Plant in Baghdad, a symbol of the vulnerability of civilians and the targeting of civilian sites in war. March 2003.

14. As CPT, we rode buses instead of planes, against the counsel of Peace Brigades International and Witness for Peace, so that we could more easily interact with armed actors in the complex, violent setting of Colombia. 2001.

15. Arlene and I have refused to pay the federal excise war tax on all phone calls. 1969–2020.

16. Our family rode bicycles, walked, and hitchhiked the first dozen years of our married life instead of owning a car. 1971–1984.

17. I participated with others in rebuilding Palestinian homes, demolished because of the strictures of the Israeli occupation. It was a positive building action in a time of unbuilding. 1995–1998.

18. With others on the Palestine CPT team, I carried out a seven-hundred-hour liquid fast to protest seven hundred Israeli demolition orders against Palestinian homes in the Hebron District. 1997.

19. Along with others on the Iraq CPT team, I did a forty-day Lenten liquid fast to protest the treatment of detainees by the US occupation in Iraq. March-April 2004.

20. CPT and Iraqi groups held a very public vigil three days per week in Tahrir Circle, Baghdad, to raise awareness of the issues of Iraqis detained by the US. 2004.

21. I participated in a silent march in San Juan, Puerto Rico, a march opposing the US Navy presence and bombing on Vieques. It was the largest march in Puerto Rican history. 2000.

22. I was a member of the Migrant Trail Walk, a seventy-mile trek from inside Mexico to Tucson, Arizona. It marked the route and agonies of those crossing the border because of economic constraints in their homes because of the NAFTA agreement or violence in their home countries. June 2004.

23. I went with CPT into Iraq, in violation of US sanctions against travel and aid, in order to nonviolently stop a war. October 2002—March 2003.

24. Jeff Heie and I as CPTers accompanied a water delivery truck to Hani Abu Heikel's home in Tel Rumeida, Hebron, Palestinian West Bank, when Israeli military and settlers wanted to stop his access to water so he would have to move. 1995.

25. Arlene and I homeschooled our two daughters with an emphasis on cross cultural experiences and used Howard Zinn's A People's History of the United States. 1983–1999.

26. In our home we built a solar cooker, a solar water heater, a composting toilet, and a wood stove water heater. 1985.

27. At Joyfield Farm we have planted many trees, for nuts, fruits, oxygen, wildlife and bird habitat, and to nurture a micro-climate for our garden. 1983–2020.

28. For our garden, we use lots of compost piles, leaves from town for mulch and compost, and horse manure with sawdust bedding to add nutrients and build up humus. It is one way to recycle waste products from the town and farms and in the process minimize the risk of drought and flooding by adding humus to our soil. 1983–2020.

29. I led a seven-member CPT delegation to the International Christian Zionist Convention in Orlando to share stories of the Israeli occupation in a space where those stories were invisible. April 29 to May 3, 1998.

30. I initiated letters, phone calls, and visits to presidents and legislators in Washington, DC, about situations in Palestine, Colombia, and Iraq.

31. Our family provided refuge for two families from Guatemala on the underground railroad. This was a period during which two hundred thousand indigenous Guatemalans were killed, assisted by US training and military aid. 1984.

32. I helped as CPT accompanied Palestinian children walking to and from school when they were being harassed by Israeli settlers. 1990s.

33. I joined a Witness for Peace delegation to Nicaragua during the US-backed Contra War as a protest of that violence. 1985.

34. After our morning worship, CPT picked up trash daily in the park at the Il Ibrihimi Mosque in Hebron. 1995–1997.

35. We held a worship time daily on benches in the park before the mosque/synagogue in Hebron, not as a diminution of either of those important faiths, but as an expression of the faith that inspired our peacemaking. 1995–1997.

36. At the invitation of the Hebron municipality, CPT cleaned up and moved into an apartment in the old city of Hebron when Palestinians were moving out under pressure from the Israeli occupation. 1995.

37. CPT talked about and taught nonviolence at Hebron University. 1995.

38. CPT worked with Fatah, the Palestinian Land Defense Committee, Rabbis for Human Rights, and World Vision on nonviolent actions against the Israeli occupation of Palestine.1995–1998.

39. We prayed for peace with Mexican immigration and military personnel at Chenalhó checkpoints in the highlands of Chiapas, Mexico. It seemed to be a clear factor in the closing of the immigration checkpoints. 1998.

40. CPT visited and reminded six different security forces in Pierre, South Dakota, that CPT was watching, and we represented over three thousand churches across North America, as those security forces were harassing the Lakota warrior peace encampment. 1999.

41. In Hebron and Iraq we in CPT, often used dirty dish and laundry water to flush toilets. Water was one of the key underlying issues of those conflicts.

42. At Joyfield, we catch rainwater off the house and barn for irrigation.

43. We have used one well and one water filter for four households at Joyfield Farm.

44. Arlene and I invited Dad and Mom Kindy to retire at Joyfield Farm instead of moving to a retirement home. We lived as neighbors. 1989–2013.

45. CPT monitored the Department of Fisheries and Oceans and the Royal Canadian Mounted Police as they harassed native lobster fishers of Esgenoopetitj First Nation in New Brunswick, Canada. 2000.

46. CPT and Voices in the Wilderness, jointly in Iraq as the Iraq Peace Team, provided an alternative voice to mainline media during the US "Shock and Awe" assault on Baghdad, Iraq. 2003.

47. CPT helped build a communication bridge between the US Paliwoda Forward Operating Base and Iraqi human rights lawyers in Balad, Iraq. January 2004.

48. CPT held a vigil with Iraqi Human Rights Watch between the Hussein and Ali Shrines in Kerbala on behalf of Iraqis detained by US forces. 2004.

49. We dramatically enlarged the size of photographs of regular Iraqi civilians and hung them from the windows of our hotels to greet US invading troops. March 2003.

50. CPT prayed with Muslims at the Khadum Shrine with Saayad Ali (Shia) and the Abu Hanifa Mosque with Sheik Moayad (Sunni), both in Baghdad. 2004–2005.

51. We use a Maytag wringer washer at our home in Joyfield to reduce water usage. 1983–2020.

52. We use a solar clothes dryer at home, and I do on CPT projects also. 1983–2020.

53. We do hand washing of dishes at home and I hand wash clothes and dishes on CPT projects. 1983–2020.

54. I did a two-hundred-mile walking pilgrimage and speaking tour from Goshen, Indiana, to Columbus, Ohio, in support of Gene Stoltzfus and Doug Pritchard as they were exploring a potential CPT project in Afghanistan. December 2001 and January 2002.

55. Michael Goode and I did a 220-mile walk from Boeing headquarters in Chicago to Caterpillar headquarters in Peoria, Illinois, as a protest of their tools being used by Israel to kill Palestinian children. 2002.

56. I carried dates from Iraq to the US as a protest of the thirteen-year US embargo of Iraqi goods. 2003.

57. I monitored Israeli military checkpoints of Palestinian people and cars with a notebook and camera. 1995–1997.

58. Often joined by other CPTers, I followed Israeli patrols on foot through the city of Hebron at night to hold them accountable for their actions. 1995–1997.

59. I helped plant tomatoes and broccoli plants on Palestinian lands threatened by expanding Israeli settlements in Hebron and Bethlehem. 1995–1997.

60. I sent frequent letters to the editor about the conflicts in Iraq, Palestine, and Colombia.

61. Dad and I did a Christmas Day vigil at the Indiana Air National Guard Base in Fort Wayne, Indiana because of the involvement of the guard in the attack on Afghanistan. 2001.

62. I joined Dave Lambert and Sox Sperry for a sit-in at the offices of Senators Lugar and Quayle in Fort Wayne, asking for dialogue, and protesting the ongoing US invasion of Nicaragua. 1985.

63. With a CPT training group, I crossed onto Extra Low Frequency (ELF) land in Ashland, Wisconsin, to protest this communication system that enabled first strike nuclear war. 1997.

64. With others, I carried baby food into Lowry Air Force Base, Denver, to ask that this be the alternative to bombs dropped on Iraq in the first gulf war. November 1990.

65. I crossed the line at the School of the Americas in Fort Benning, Georgia, to protest US torture training of Latin America police and military. 2000.

66. I entered the cruise missile factory with Ken Brown at Walled Lake, Michigan, to protest their deployment and threatened use across Europe. 1992.

67. I visited the Canal Zone in Panama to protest US military operations from that center. 1976.

68. I went into Fort Bragg military base in North Carolina to protest the training of Salvadoran troops and invite those troops to leave. 1987.

69. I turned in my draft card to protest Selective Service facilitation of the war in Vietnam. 1970.

70. I left my approved project as a conscientious objector to protest the Vietnam War. I continued my two-year commitment to Brethren Volunteer Service. 1970–1971.

71. I had a short dialogue about the draft and the Vietnam War with Curtis Tarr, head of Selective Service, on the Phil Donahue Show. 1970.

72. Our BVS project household offered hospitality for an AWOL Vietnam veteran on his way to the Winter Soldier Investigation in Detroit. It was a public trial of that increasingly unpopular war, even among military personnel. 1970.

73. I assisted in draft counseling young people during the Vietnam War and during the reinstatement of the draft during President Carter's response to the holding of hostages in Tehran, Iran.

74. I encourage young people to refuse to cooperate with the draft or Selective Service System.

75. I invited Israeli soldiers to consider leaving their military assignments in the occupied territories of Palestine because of the negative impact of the occupation on Palestinians and themselves. 1995–1997.

76. Arlene and I converted a drive through corn crib into a home at Joy-field Farm. 1985–2020.

77. At Joyfield Farm, we installed thirty-six solar panels on the barn roof to encourage an alternative energy to coal or nuclear power. 2010.

78. Arlene and I chose to stop working at Goshen Rubber when we discovered they had a defense contract. 1970s.

Appendix C:
War Blogs, Nigeria

I REALIZE THAT MANY readers of this book do not have experience in conflict zones. I have chosen to include this selection of short blogs from a three-month period, December 2014 through February 2015, while I was working in Nigeria with Brethren Disaster Ministries through the Crisis Management Team of Ekklesiyar Yan'uwa a Nigeria (EYN). Since it includes specific stories of people and events that erupted from the conflict raging in Nigeria at the time, I think it will provide a clearer understanding of the breadth and complexity of a war zone.

A ROCKY BEGINNING

The EYN church at Vinikilang was the first city congregation, as EYN intentionally expanded from the country and the smaller villages in 1978. That meeting place is a large structure in the shape of a cross, with roof trusses built like others I have seen only near North Manchester, as in a former barn of Harold and Rosemary Bolinger. The space will hold up to fifteen hundred people easily. [One pastor noted that the smallest of twelve churches Boko Haram had leveled, as they completely destroyed his district, was larger than Vinikilang.] This structure is built on a massive outcropping of rock that rises above the Benue River, which cuts through this eastern portion of Nigeria. Owen Shankster was the designer/builder of the church.

Vinikilang #1 was the site of the first trauma healing workshop led by Reverend Toma Ragnjiya and his assistant Dlama Kagula. Providing opportunities to heal from the trauma, implicit in the tragedy that has overwhelmed EYN, is one focus of the Crisis Management Team. Reverend Toma has taken on this task as director of the Peace Program of EYN.

Thirty-four mostly displaced pastors were there for this three-day workshop on top of the rock. Themes of the training ranged from stress, trauma, anger, and grief, to trust and healing from trauma, with ample time for sharing personal experiences with each other. Stress, anger, and grief are normal human emotions, but trauma is an emotional experience that overwhelms the human capacity to recover. What are the steps that help individuals and groups move through trauma to trust, acceptance, and healing? How can pastors facilitate that process for their families, congregations, and communities?

At the end of the first day, one pastor noted, "My blood pressure has dropped significantly. I am no longer carrying immense anger toward Boko Haram." Leadership had invited participants to imagine Boko Haram fighters also dealing with trauma, perhaps sitting with them in the same circle.

Reverend Toma estimates that trauma has impacted hundreds of thousands of people in EYN alone. There is a long road ahead for their communities in northeast Nigeria, but these first steps were taken before Christmas 2014, on the rocky outcropping above the Benue River near Yola.

BUILDING A TRAUMA HEALING MODEL FOR NIGERIA

In EYN alone there may be two hundred thousand to six hundred thousand people impacted by trauma. But across Nigeria the violence of Boko Haram has displaced one and a half million people, according to reports. Are all of them dealing with trauma issues that need some major healing? How can a program be put together to deal with that level of need?

In Rwanda in 1994, about one million people died in very brutal fashion in one hundred days. It was primarily an ethnic divide within communities. The Society of Friends (Quakers) has been instrumental in shaping an excellent community-based trauma healing program that has been used extensively in Rwanda, Burundi, and the Democratic Republic of the Congo, and today is being planted in the Central African Republic.

But the division here in Nigeria is not ethnic. It is also not religious. And it is not based in communities since the attackers come in from the outside. Different groups in Nigeria have been doing trauma workshops to help people move beyond their trauma to face a more positive future. All of these models have their own strengths, but is there a model that will fit Nigeria across faith lines . . . that works in IDP (internally displaced persons) camps . . . which can be used where IDPs are living in the homes of families and friends . . . or with those who have escaped Boko Haram, or have been living in the bush?

On January 26–29, 2015, twenty-four trauma healing practitioners came together with these questions facing them. Mennonite Central Committee (MCC) supplied funding for this effort. Some practitioners had received training from the Rwanda model. Some used a specifically Christian format. Others had gone through other trauma training courses. Carefronting, a program which had been doing peacebuilding and trauma programs in Nigeria and across the Americas and Europe, led the sessions.

EYN will soon have five individuals trained under the Rwanda model. While the Peace Committee of EYN was leading trauma workshops in Yola, Jalingo, and Abuja, some trainees clearly stood out in terms of interest and ability, so they would be good to include on a trauma healing team. Maybe ten of the group involved in the late January Carefronting sessions would be free to assist as part of a strengthened team. MCC has one person who could be freed up. Perhaps twenty-five or thirty people could form a group to increase the capacity of a trauma training group to tackle the needs of EYN—at least for nine hundred people!

MCC is also funding a three-day trauma workshop for staff of EYN. These are the folks who have not only experienced the trauma of losing their churches and homes but have been displaced and still keep serving the needs of a devastated church. That workshop happened in Jos the first week of February.

Soon, MCC is funding a program on trauma for the pastors of EYN. Likely that will happen in at least two locations, as pastors gather for their yearly meetings. Clearly, the staff and pastors will be part of the response by EYN to the traumatization of a denomination. But what will the capacity-building of trained persons to carry this across the church look like?

Once the three new trainees return from Rwanda and some workshops happen around Abuja there will be about thirty people ready to shape into the trauma healing team. They will all probably go through a more extensive training for trauma healers with Carefronting. Then, as teams of two trainees in each leadership group, they will work as assistants with the skilled Carefronting trainers as they hold two trauma healing workshops of thirty people each. Then the leadership teams of two will lead their own workshops two times under the supervision of the trained Carefronting leaders. Once they go through this entire process, 1200 to 1800 hundred people will have gone through the workshops at the point the thirty trainees would be ready to move on their own!

These trained trauma healing people could be sent to different settings across the country. Those could be IDP camps focusing on children or villages with a focus on the women who hold families together. Or they might work with young people who have been kidnapping targets by Boko Haram seeking wives or recruits for a new generation of fighters.

In our broken world it seems that trauma that is not dealt with reappears as another manifestation that traumatizes with violence another population. An example is Jewish Israelis who experienced the horrors of the Holocaust and today have imposed a new disaster on Palestine. As people of faith we need to continually discover ways to end the repeating cycle of violence and trauma. This growing development of a Nigerian trauma healing model is clearly a strong new step in that direction.

CHIBOK

April 14, 2014, Boko Haram raided the community of Chibok, Borno State, and kidnapped nearly 300 women students from their boarding school. In spite of the world outcry of horror, most of those young women are still abducted and their whereabouts are unknown. But that event was not the only time that this community and region has been impacted by Boko Haram.

According to the EYN District Church Council (DCC) secretary, Reverend Bitrus Jidda, the problems started in November 2012. It was then that Boko Haram gunmen attacked and burned the police headquarters in Chibok. They continued to the EYN congregation of Kwaple, where they killed Reverend Michael Peter and nine of the church members. The attackers also burned their homes and belongings.

In December, two days after Christmas, Boko Haram attacked the EYN congregation of Kulali where they burned the church, parsonage and some homes.

Then in June 2013, gunmen burned three more EYN churches and the houses in the same district. Twenty EYN members lost their lives in this raid. Then on November 13, Boko Haram returned to Chibok about 4:00 p.m. They destroyed three more EYN churches. Though mosques have been burned and attacked by Boko Haram in other parts of the northeast, this region is predominantly Christian and nearly all the Christians are EYN. EYN churches and members have been the primary victims in this region.

There are thirteen congregations in the Chibok district. Despite the assaults, at least nine of the congregations have members that are still regularly meeting for worship. Over 500 were in attendance at the one church in Chibok itself. There are four churches where the district secretary is unsure whether members are meeting. This is the reality, despite the fact that Boko Haram essentially controls all of the region around Chibok, including the roads. The Nigerian military is only in Chibok itself and the nearby community of Damboa. Even neighboring EYN center Lassa remains under Boko Haram control.

In a closely neighboring EYN district, there have been two recent Boko Haram attacks. Boko Haram killed fifteen EYN members last week in Kautikari town. Just before that, they burned most of the homes of members in the newly-organized Gwagwamdi EYN church, just ten kilometers away from Chibok.

On the heels of the April kidnapping, fifty of the women escaped from their captors. While 172 of the original kidnapped women were EYN, twenty-nine of the escapees were EYN. Some of those twenty-nine are still living in Chibok, some have accepted invitations to schooling in the US, and some have been assisted by the Interfaith Adamawa Peace Initiative in preparing for examinations that were interrupted by the kidnapping. At this time, the story does not have an ending.

DISEMPOWERMENT AS AN IDP— ASABE JOHN MAMZZA BAZZA

Being an internally displaced person in Nigeria means that one is no longer able to live in one's own home. Here in Nigeria, 1,500,000 persons have become displaced because of the attacks and threats from Boko Haram. Having to relocate to another place might entail moving to the home of friends or family who are quite welcoming. It might mean living in the bush where conditions might be minimal, but a higher level of security is felt. Or it might mean settling into a camp where there are many other IDPs and some level of support from non-governmental organizations (NGOs) or government.

Yesterday I talked more extensively with Asabe John Mamzza Bazza, an IDP who is living here at the Catholic Retreat Center in Yola. Through marriage, she is connected with the bishop of this region and was invited to live here with her extended family when Boko Haram took over her village. She and her family are from EYN. Her father, Reverend Ilya, was a pastor in Lassa.

She has been here for five months. At home she would be busy with tasks that care for her family. Here she sits and waits for food to be given to her. She and her relatives spend the day moving their mats from one shady spot to another, as the scorching sun moves across the day. She waits for clothes to be provided for her needs, because she had to flee with just what she was wearing. She says she feels she has no power.

At home she has her own garden. If she needs food, she goes "to pick the food, cashews, lemons, groundnuts" to feed her family. If she needs clothes, she has them in her house or can sell farm produce or animals for money to buy them. She has resources to purchase school supplies for her children.

Here she feels unable to help others, her family or neighbors. She is without the resources that are so available to her at home. This city is a strange place where she does not have access. At home she has connections, but here she is rootless and powerless.

What does this feeling of powerlessness do over a long period? One begins to feel very small and helpless. A recognition of total dependency on others builds a new reality. Where one had been self-reliant and quite independent, one becomes incapable of changing the dynamics that impact one's life. The larger problems appear beyond one's influence. The problem of violence from Boko Haram seems untouchable. And even the smaller issues begin to appear like mountains.

Prayer? Her prayer that Boko Haram would be stopped before reaching her village was not answered. Her prayer that her needs would be met in a positive way seems to be answered only minimally. Her prayer that the threat of Boko Haram would be eradicated by the government so she could return home has seemingly not even been heard. Despair starts to set into her life. Does God even care?

The monotony of life here at the Center is nothing like her life in the village. There she can constantly influence her future. Here she has few ways to change her future. Living door-to-door here with other IDPs who are similarly disempowered and dependent makes her feel small and worthless.

Later in the evening, one of her neighbors exploded with anger for the entire neighborhood to listen in to the family squabble. Having no diversions of work or community activity allows tensions to build between people until they explode. Are there networks of healing in this place?

GRACE

Rev. Tsiabari and Martha are both from Lassa, the second mission location of the Church of the Brethren in Nigeria. He has been pastor at EYN Mishara Para in the Uba District. They have three daughters and two sons. As these stories usually go, the family had to leave their home when fighting by Boko Haram reached their community. They fled first to Yola and then to Jalingo, where they are presently living with another pastor and his family.

Their daughter Grace is seventeen years old. She had been top of her class when her world fell apart with the family displacement. She is deaf, having lost her hearing when she was four. Displacement means the family is without income and unable to place her in a school. School has been stopped/interrupted for most of the displaced children because teachers are displaced, schools have sometimes been destroyed, and there are few students in their original communities.

The government has essentially decided to close those schools for this crisis time. The Crisis Management Team of EYN has the responsibility to figure out a way for some education to continue for the displaced school children without overriding the government decision. For Grace, the situation is compounded by her hearing loss. What happens to Grace?

KWAJAFFA EYN DISTRICT

The Kwajaffa District is situated between Biu and Garkida, both areas under the control of the Nigerian military. The Kwajaffa region is under the control of Boko Haram.

That control by Boko Haram has led to the killing of fifteen EYN members and the kidnapping of six more, including the wife and son of the EYN pastor of the Kwajaffa-2 local congregation.

Ten of the EYN churches in this district are burned to the ground. The attacks started in September and October. The most recent burning was the third week of January. At that time Boko Haram also burned many EYN shops and homes.

It appears that pressure against Boko Haram to the east of this district in the Mubi/Michika area and to the north in Maiduguri has pushed Boko Haram into these more rural areas around Kwajaffa. Without Nigerian military protection in this district, and with the increasing inability to attack with ease elsewhere, it appears Boko Haram is venting its frustration on areas like Kwajaffa.

OMEGA DOUDA

Omega Douda visited the EYN offices in Jos today. He had come from a refugee camp in Cameroon. But his travels had started in July from the village of Wagga.

Omega, his wife, and four children saw over a dozen police fleeing from their base near Wagga, in front of a widespread attack by Boko Haram in neighboring communities. The family had time to gather themselves and some belongings before traveling together into Cameroon. Initially, there were 2,000 refugees from those scattered communities that took the brunt of the Boko Haram raid. Both Muslims and Christians settled in Tura Camp though refugees from Gwoza had landed there first since it was attacked earlier.

The Cameroon government has provided support for the camp. Since the news from Nigeria has not been good in recent months, many of the refugees have moved back away from the border to settle permanently in this new country. There have been recent raids across the border by Boko Haram, so a greater distance from the border provides more protection. There is also less likelihood that Cameroon soldiers will mistake refugee individuals in the bush as Boko Haram and kill them, as has happened to some EYN members.

Presently there is a group of 400 EYN members in Tura Camp. Omega plans to return there shortly, and his family has decided they will settle in Cameroon. Some of the Cameroon communities where IDPs have settled have designated pastors and Omega and his family are part of one of those more established EYN churches.

REVEREND LUKA TADA NDAWALA

Reverend Luka Tada Ndawala explains he is the district secretary for Attagara District of EYN and is from Attagara Village. On June 3, 2014, Boko Haram raided Attagara. Sixty-eight people died in the attack and sixty-five of them were from EYN. The raiders burned seven churches including the only EYN congregation. Unfortunately, the other eleven churches in his district fell to the flames of Boko Haram, as well as most of the EYN churches in the three neighboring districts.

Reverend Luka fled across the border to Cameroon while his wife and children fled to Michika. When Michika came under attack in early September, the family reunited in Cameroon. Their new home was the refugee camp, Minawwau Godola, run by the United Nations. There were 30,000 neighbors in their new home. The well that supplied the camp ran dry, the nearby river is without water now during the dry season, and the nearest village is far enough away that those going for water may choose to stay overnight.

The UN sometimes only brings enough food for seven thousand people, so the community has been good and shared what is available. The camp is far enough from the border that Boko Haram raids into Cameroon have not reached the camp, but security officials from Cameroon recently rounded up nine people from the camp they accused of being Boko Haram.

People want to return to Nigeria, but there continues to be very high risk in their home communities. Boko Haram dumped dead bodies in the wells of Attagara. All the homes are burned there. Even if Boko Haram leaves, will they plant explosives as they depart? What about the family members who joined Boko Haram and choose to live in Attagara? But how long will Cameroon continue to host these visitors in the UN camp? Is there a safe place to go in Nigeria?

Most EYN refugees are farmers and would be willing to stay in Cameroon. Reverend Luka plans to visit the government to see if there is a large plot of land where the refugees could settle and farm. He also wants to find some smaller plots to build five EYN churches. He has decided to stay in Cameroon and work with the church.

There are 15,000 EYN members in the camp. Since the camp is divided into five wards or sections, each ward has an EYN congregation that numbers about three thousand people. There are three ordained EYN pastors and twenty-three evangelists very engaged in the life of these congregations. There have been fifty-three baptisms and 235 births among the EYN members. Their neighbors in the camp are about 9,000 Catholics, 4,000 Muslims and about 2,000 Christians from other denominations. Are you interested in helping to plant new EYN churches in Cameroon?

THE VULNERABLE ONES

On Sunday, Reverend Toma gave a rousing pep talk about trauma healing during the worship service. That was appropriate since he was in the second day of the second three-day trauma workshop for pastors who are displaced. After the service, two women from EYN approached him separately.

The first was crying. She had a one-year-old daughter in a wrap on her back and an eight-year-old son nearby. She explained that she was displaced, living with her husband's family in Jalingo, where she knew no one. Her husband had just called her from Lagos, telling her that he was divorcing her and she would have to move from his family's home. What could she do? Where could she go?

The second woman was older. She had in recent years married a widower whose wife had died. The husband had just informed her that she was divorced because she had not given him any children. She also is displaced, living in a strange city.

The crisis facing EYN—violence, death, burning of homes and churches, displacement, loss of leadership—has caused serious psychological trauma for thousands in the church. Trauma can upend families. The most vulnerable are often the most invisible. Women and children bear the brunt of the crisis. What will happen to them?

ACCIDENT

An accident is an accident, right? Let me share the details of the one we had last Saturday and let you be the judge.

Dlama Kagula and I were traveling down a good stretch of highway for a change when the left front tire became unconnected at the tie rod and axle. Frankly, I thought we had been hit by an IED—it was like an explosion and the windshield shattered. The wheel and still-intact tire hit an oncoming car, our vehicle fell to the left because of the missing tire, and we crashed along the side of the passing vehicle.

The other vehicle was able to come to an upright stop even though the driver had sustained a broken left leg. Dlama somehow kept our vehicle upright, as it went off the road, made a sweeping gentle curve, and came to a stop near a shade tree. We stepped out of the car checking ourselves but were uninjured.

We saw the other car in the distance, and many passersby were gathering around it and us. In the heavily populated south of Nigeria, people pass without stopping; here in the arid, lightly populated Middle Belt of Nigeria, everyone stops. Dlama asked a motorbike driver to call the police, and he then called EYN administration in Jos. They suggested we contact the nearest EYN Church in Bauchi, but because of distance we did not. We took pictures of the damage, and by then police had arrived. The chief himself had arrived, since Alkaleri was just two or three kilometers away. In addition, a road safety crew came, and vigilantes in their own vehicle. The latter were there to maintain peace at the accident site, though there were no issues.

Before this, a passing vehicle had loaded in the other driver and taken him to the nearby general hospital, just about four kilometers distant. We got into the police vehicle and were taken directly to the hospital so we could check on the other driver.

He was on a bed just inside the door, so we were able to greet him and ask how he felt. It seems the vigilantes were also there with the police to maintain calm. The doctor arrived and pronounced that it was a simple fracture without need of an x-ray.

The other driver's father also arrived and asked that his son just be allowed to return home and they would wrap the leg and use traditional healing to allow a cure. Dlama paid the hospital for the driver's care and we were driven back to the police station.

There the police investigator who had checked the accident scene had the two of us, along with the father of the driver and owner of the other car, sit on benches around his desk. Dlama explained that he had already paid the hospital and offered to pay the towing costs to get both vehicles to the larger city of Bauchi, which would have a good repair garage. The interchanges were congenial and shortly we headed outside to catch a taxi ride on to Jos, since our vehicle was no longer usable. At this point, either the towing price increased by one fifth or the police wanted a cut.

In two days, Dlama and Markus Gamache returned to Alkaleri and received a police escort to visit the other driver again. He was doing well. They also made arrangements to pay repair costs of the other vehicle and tried to decide what to do with our vehicle. The other car was being used to generate income to complete its purchase payment, so the owner did not want it out of commission for long.

Roads in Nigeria, especially ones I have traveled on in seven or eight states, are not kept up well. Huge and frequent potholes turn driving into a motorsport event. The condition of the roadways has a major impact on the condition of vehicles. Many damaged vehicles find homes along the road-sides, and accidents are frequent as high-speed swerves cause drivers to lose control of the vehicles. We had experienced many holes that should have destroyed our suspension, but a smooth roadway was where our gear finally gave up. It was a well-built Toyota like many other quality vehicles on the highway, but this time and space was its moment to fail.

CCEPI DISTRIBUTION

On December 10, the Center for Caring, Empowerment, and Peace Initiatives (CCEPI) team gathered food supplies at the Boulder Hill compound which houses the temporary headquarters of EYN in Jos. Displaced families had gathered and were already registered, for ease in distribution. CCEPI is one of the EYN-connected NGOs that is being funded by Brethren Disaster Ministries through its Nigeria Crisis Relief appeal.

There was a rope outlining the area for supplies and for the CCEPI team to operate. Rebecca Dali, Director of the NGO, called out names. As families came to the rope, each family received a plastic bucket, a large mat, twenty kilograms of maize, a blanket, two soaps, and a bag of beans.

It was a colorful scene with bright scarves, children being nursed, other children playing in the clusters of people, a corner of elderly folks sitting patiently to receive some assistance, and other hopeful, unregistered displaced folks waiting to see if supplies would stretch for them as well.

In the background, the regular routine of the busy compound continued its usual pattern. EYN staff were in and out of their offices, which were being spruced up with furniture to allow a more functional facility. A private school had delivered a huge load of relief supplies to the headquarters earlier that day. There were stacks of toiletries, yams, dried food goods, and other edibles ready for distribution to the people displaced from the northeast of Nigeria.

Back at the rope around the CCEPI distribution circles, people were sharing with each other. An EYN pastor from Michika, who had been hit by three bullets as Boko Haram moved into his home area in September, was there, still healing. Although he had not registered, he was hoping supplies would stretch to him.

A Church of Christ pastor and his wife were among those waiting. He had just finished an office management course and was returning home when Boko Haram reached his region. The family fled to Yola and then on to Jos, when rumors of an impending attack on Yola spread. He was the one in the crowd advocating for a group of elderly patiently waiting at the edge of the circle. It seemed these elders were not on the registration list, and he wanted them to get first opportunity at any extra supplies.

The distribution went smoothly for the over 100 families. Having it off the road in a closed area with sufficient staff facilitated the process. Only a singing ZME choir (EYN women's group) would have improved the setting!

CRISIS MANAGEMENT TEAM

The Standing Committee of EYN has commissioned a seven-member Crisis Management Team to coordinate the church's response to the overwhelming disaster that has engulfed EYN, especially in northeast Nigeria. Though the disaster has been years in developing, this year, 2014, has been an especially difficult year for the church.

In April, Boko Haram abducted over 300 women students, 170 EYN, from their school in Chibok. Through the summer there were more attacks by Boko Haram in EYN areas of Borno, Adamawa, and Yobe states. Then on October 29, the EYN headquarters and Kulp Bible College had to evacuate as Boko Haram ransacked Mubi and the surrounding area.

In August Jay Wittmeyer and Roy Winter of the Church of the Brethren (COB) met with the EYN Standing Committee and drew up a detailed response plan to the crisis. By November, though the framework of the plan remained valid, the crisis had grown immensely.

Carl and Roxane Hill were in Nigeria encouraging the process as the Team members were selected and the Standing Committee commissioned them for the work. It wasn't just a simple two-step plan that confronted the Team.

Their task included: 1) providing emergency feeding for tens of thousands of displaced, with a focus on EYN families, but recognizing the need to assist others where populations are mixed; 2) selecting leadership to carry out/coordinate an extensive trauma healing process for the church; 3) assisting with the re-establishment of an EYN headquarters, for this time an annex in Jos at the Boulder Hill property, and a new setting for Kulp Bible College on EYN land near Chinka; 4) organizing the return of thousands of EYN members from the refugee camps and the mountains of Cameroon; 5) settling refugees who would not return to their original homes onto newly purchased locations with homes, school, clinic and place of worship; 6) quickly moving formerly-displaced families from a dependence on emergency food to a position of being able to sustain themselves through jobs and farming; 7) expanding the peacebuilding work of EYN; and 8) carrying out regular advocacy with embassies and other potential partners in the relief efforts.

Implicit in this relief task was the vision to grow EYN as a national and international church. Developing the headquarters annex in Jos moved the center of the church to a location more easily accessible to the rest of Nigeria and neighboring countries. With Kulp Bible College in Chinka, that central accessibility for leadership training also holds true. When the return to Mubi is possible, these new developments will provide for increased opportunities for church growth.

In December, both the COB and Mission-21 (formerly Basel Mission) made initial commitments to be partners with EYN in this immense undertaking. Mission-21 has been sending mission workers and financial support for EYN since Basel Mission merged with EYN in 1962, so this partnership is just a more explicit commitment to support the response to this disaster. One of the complicating factors for this three-way partnership is that the disaster continues with no indication that it will cease.

Support from the Church of the Brethren is essential. Major fundraising will be required and many volunteers will be needed to walk with EYN in this process. It is a massive undertaking for all three of the partners.

DR. SAFIYA JOHANNA BYO

Dr. Safiya Johanna Byo is Director of Education for EYN. She has been in that position for two years and has grabbed onto the tasks with zeal. During the 1970s, Nigeria took over all the schools which EYN had developed. EYN had in place a very strong program in education and the government apparently needed that level of quality.

In the intervening years, government educational institutions have not kept pace with what is possible. EYN has slowly developed their own private schools. Kulp Bible College and three bible schools are under the responsibility of EYN. Many of the districts have their own bible schools and are responsible for their grant programs. Dr. Safiya distributes scholarships for deserving students to the four schools under EYN jurisdiction.

EYN has about forty primary schools and five secondary schools that were operating, but now many of those are unable to operate because of the conflict. Dr. Safiya is responsible for building the teaching capacity for the teachers in these schools. This is a huge and ongoing task given the numbers of teachers involved.

A third area of responsibility for Dr. Safiya is Sunday School (SS) teachers. Should SS teachers be trained? How important is the religious education of our children? Dr. Safiya answers these questions with an emphatic, "Yes!" and a strong "Very!" There is now in place a guideline book for SS teachers and a songbook to be used as a supplement for classroom activities. This last year, there was a retreat for representatives of the SS teachers from each of the fifty districts in EYN.

Preaching was at the base of that retreat since teachers who aren't grounded in their own strong discipleship won't be able to pass on good faith training to their students. In addition, there was skill empowerment training in areas like farming, saving money, animals, and sustainable economic models.

This year Dr. Safiya had decided to do a very intensive two-week training with the teacher representatives. Then the displacement of the headquarters placed a huge kink in those plans.

But the massive displacement among EYN brought to the forefront a two-pronged fourth responsibility that Dr. Safiya has shouldered. Displacement has usually meant that any worship or education programs have stopped. Before two months had passed after the displacement, Dr. Safiya had trained twenty-two people as teachers in the unusual settings of IDP camps or church compounds where many displaced families found their new residence. Working with three different congregational sites and four IDP camp locations around Jos, Dr. Safiya has set in place Sunday School programs, with trained teachers for the children who have been displaced from their homes.

In two of those sites, regular school classes have already begun to meet during the week, since the government has been unable to provide schooling for displaced children. Again the church is in the vanguard of forging new models of education to meet the needs of children.

As a second prong of her response to displacement, Dr. Safiya understands that trauma is part of the school baggage carried by each displaced child who is a student. She is concerned for the children to have opportunities to heal from the trauma of the violence and displacement to which they have been subjected. She plans to work with the EYN Peace Committee to grapple with this much larger issue.

Dr. Safiya had her training in Nigeria, Kenya and the United States. One additional piece readers should understand is that she was also displaced from the EYN Headquarters October 29, 2014, with the Boko Haram attack. She fled first to Yola and had to deal with her abandoned office and traumatized secretary. She then transferred to the new Annex in Jos, while preparing for her own wedding last December! Can you begin to sense the load carried by EYN staff like Dr. Safiya?

GHOMBA DUTSE CAMP

The EYN Crisis Management Team visited a group of internally displaced (IDP) families on the outskirts of Abuja, the capital of Nigeria, for a distribution of basic food supplies. The distribution included basics like choice of guinea corn or rice, cooking oil, salt, sugar, and tea, supplemented with salve, laundry and hand soap. Most of the thirty-eight families—144 people—were from EYN.

The Team met them under a grove of trees, where the significant presence of visitors attracted a group of youth on motorbikes hoping to gain some benefits as well. One of the complications in distribution is cordoning off a space so that those who are the neediest really are the beneficiaries, without causing problems that haunt the recipients after the donors depart.

These Ghomba Dutse Camp EYN families are spending nights on the concrete floors of fancy new empty homes. These are part of the many new housing additions springing up as speculators try to cash in on increasing demand for housing with Abuja's growth. Families sleep in certain homes while youth stay in nearby homes. Often in cases like this, a displaced person pays the night guards fifty Naira (about thirty cents) per night for the privilege of doing this in housing additions or public schools. The night squatters need to be out by five in the morning before school staff or construction workers return to their sites.

There are reports that property owners call in the military to shoot squatters in situations like this one the Team visited. The raids often result in deaths and of course make it even more difficult for displaced families to find a space to live.

One of the NGOs that is funded by Brethren Disaster Ministries has offered to take the most vulnerable of the families in Ghomba Dutse Camp and incorporate them into the already organized resettlement community near Gurku. Have you ever been displaced and homeless with no resources?

GURKU LIFELINE INTERFAITH CAMP FOOD DISTRIBUTION

Early in the morning of December 13, a panel truck left Abuja loaded with food supplies collected by the Crisis Management Team of EYN. It traveled to the Gurku community and the setting for a food distribution to sixty-six displaced families, 404 people. This is a group of displaced Muslim and Christian families representing many languages, tribes, and villages. The Lifeline Compassionate Global Initiatives (LCGI) staff is nurturing this re-settlement. Lifeline is an intentional interfaith effort that intends to bridge the growing divide between Christians and Muslims in Nigeria.

The EYN Team had already distributed food to the camps at Gongola and Ghomba Dutse the day before. Those deliveries were complicated by many people who appeared at the distribution who were not displaced and were already living in the area.

The setting for this food distribution was the compound of a local family that had rented space to many of the displaced families. It was well off the road and blessed with the shade of many trees. The shelter from other travelers-by meant the distribution would not be interrupted by inquisitive neighbors.

Folks had already gathered but waited patiently as supplies were unloaded. A tiger swallowtail butterfly greeted the newcomers and the stacks of supplies. The butterfly remained in the area checking in throughout the morning.

Each family received its choice of fifty kilograms of guinea corn or rice, cooking oil, noodles, bouillon cubes, salt, sugar, and tea, as well as laundry soap, hand soap, and salve. While the adult distribution was happening, the children were receiving packages of nutritious crackers. The delivery project went smoothly that morning with a good spirit permeating the clusters of people.

Nine of the families in the camp still have husbands displaced in Cameroon. There is a concentrated effort to enable them to return shortly, because they are sorely missed by their families. A building project that provides land, homes, a school, medical clinic, and worship spaces for both Muslim and Christian worshipers has started, with ambitious plans to complete the project by the end of March—the likely start of the rainy season. This effort is funded in part by assistance from Brethren Disaster Ministries. LCGI is recognized under the EYN umbrella but is an independent NGO which is providing an excellent model of resettlement for mixed religious communities.

MAIDUGURI

The city of Maiduguri in Borno State has parts of two different EYN districts within its boundaries. There are six large EYN congregations within the city, with the main Maiduguri congregation attracting five thousand people for worship. EYN is the largest Christian group in that region and is one of three denominations indigenous to that part of the country. The city and the city churches have expanded rapidly with the recent attacks by Boko Haram in Baga, on the shore of Lake Chad.

There had been a local EYN congregation in Baga itself at the time of the destruction of the city by Boko Haram. There were many other EYN congregations and preaching points in the areas around Baga. Those have been among the small communities raided and burned by Boko Haram. Refugees have fled into Chad, Niger, and Cameroon for safety. Many also fled into the more secure city of Maiduguri.

EYN has a well-coordinated response to the crisis within the city. There are three Christian IDP camps within the city limits and six Muslim IDP camps. Most of the Christians are staying with families and friends, so as many as seventy people are with some of the families. Although not all the displaced are registered, today (Saturday) there were a total of 45,858 Christian IDPs registered in the city, and there are probably close to a similar number of Muslims in the six camps. That number has increased nearly threefold from before Christmas and is growing rapidly each day. Federal and state governments have been providing assistance to the IDP camps, and the organization of the Christian community has seemed to cover those IDPs staying with families who are missed by the government distributions.

Security within the city is very tight. Persons going to markets or churches are closely screened. Metal detecting wands scan each person at churches before entry. If there is any question, people are patted down. No packages are allowed inside the church. A bible is the only thing attendees are allowed to carry with them. The Holy Spirit is the only thing that can pass through security unimpeded. That Spirit seems to be present in abundance as churches are growing under the pressure.

Updates are coming in. Today (Sunday) Maiduguri was being attacked by Boko Haram from three directions. In the east, they were thirty kilometers away; in the north, 130 kilometers away; and the west, ten kilometers away. People inside said it sounded like shooting was from all directions. An EYN pastor in Jos has three children in school in Maiduguri and they were the ones that called in the first reports. The city ordered all people to stay indoors so that the military would know who was attacking. The markets were closed. Latest reports are that the military repelled the attacks against Maiduguri, but that a city to the west with Nigerian military barracks did fall to the attackers. Clearly, Boko Haram wants everyone to think they are everywhere and able to attack successfully wherever they choose.

PEACE AND DEMOCRACY CONFERENCE

The Peace Committee of EYN started in 2002 and is now under the leadership of Dr. Toma Ragnjiwi. One emphasis of the Peace Committee was to strengthen relationships between Muslims and Christians. Out of that effort came CAMPI, Christians and Muslims Peacebuilding Initiative, in 2010. One of their projects in 2012 was to begin Peace Clubs in the schools of the Mubi area. Peace Clubs there developed with a strong mix of Muslim and Christian students and sponsors.

Last summer, CAMPI members visited nine Mubi schools, four public and five private, to check in on the peace clubs. The schools were excited to host the CAMPI visits, and in all but one of the schools, the club was active. Administrators were praising the club activities for reducing conflict between the religious groups in the schools.

Elections in Nigeria can often be a stimulus for violence. So CAMPI felt that a conference before the election this year with a focus on youth leaders promoting good citizenship would be an important step. It was to take place last fall, but the late October Boko Haram attack on Mubi derailed the plans.

With nine members in attendance, CAMPI met early this week and moved efficiently to: set a venue; choose a date; select speakers; prepare for security; decide how to choose which one hundred young people to invite; and affirm the topic which had been selected in the fall.

So the conference, "Peace and Democracy: Promoting Civic Responsibility," was set for Wednesday, February 11, at the government basic education lecture hall in Jimeta, Yola, Adamawa State. This was three days before the election. The Muslim youth organization was asked to choose twenty-three young people from all the local governments in the state while the ecumenical Christian organization does the same. The Union of Road Transport Workers, the members of CAMPI, and another interfaith group, Adamawa Peace Initiative are also selecting strong youth leaders, with an intentional mix of faith and gender.

Mubi is in the northern part of Adamawa State, and the four main political parties in the state have each been asked to choose a youth leader and woman leader. All these representatives will help assure that word gets out across the state about peaceful ways to effectively participate in the election.

The speakers are Hajiya Turai Kadir, a Muslim professor at American University in Yola, and Dr. Kwabi, a Christian who headed a commission at the federal level. So the speakers model the mix of gender and faiths, setting the foundation for positive participation in the electoral process. This event is one of many across Nigeria trying to set the stage for a violence-free election.

News break: Now with the election delayed for six more weeks this conference will also be postponed until before the election in March. CAMPI has not yet selected the new date for the conference.

RICH DAY

The three-member Brethren Disaster Ministries (BDM) team and the four-member Mission 21 team ate breakfast early to head out to the building project site of the Lifeline Compassionate Global Initiatives (LCGI). LCGI is an interfaith nonprofit focusing presently on this effort to house those displaced by the attacks of Boko Haram in northeast Nigeria.

Samuel Dali, who participated in the dedication, is president of EYN. He estimates that as many as 170,000 EYN members may be presently displaced from their homes as a result of the conflict ravaging northeast Nigeria. But many other Christians and many Muslims are also displaced by that fighting.

So Marcus Gamache, the spark plug for LCGI, and the LCGI committee have been building relationships, buying land, registering the sixty-three families and 394 people with the Nigeria security office, and securing funding so that today's dedication service could move ahead. Those are the families and people who will settle this newly-purchased farmland. The community will lie on the edge of the rugged foothills of the mountains on the north edge of Abuja, the capital of Nigeria.

One might assume that since Boko Haram says it is Muslim, displaced EYN members might not welcome a home next to a Muslim family. But this interfaith planning group has realized that building good relationships across faith lines is one way to break down those animosities that lead to war.

BDM and Mission-21 have funded and encouraged the efforts of LCGI. A line of men and women, some of the ones who will soon move into these homes, carried blocks from where they were formed, down the road to the first home where they became the foundation. A bore hole will be dug next week to provide the water needed for this large construction project. Marcus estimates that the community of homes should be completed by March.

Four EYN pastors and their families are among the new settlers. A worship center for Muslims and one for Christians will be part of this new community. Spiritual undergirding will be essential for this new beginning.

This is a small start, with thousands of people yet to settle, but the LCGI committee trusts this site will provide a model that will inspire others. The riches of God are new every morning.

VISIONS IN THE NIGHT

One year ago, the Wagga community had a population of between four and five thousand people. Last summer, July 13, the population increased by three to five hundred as Boko Haram attacked in cars and on motorbikes. From that point the population dropped precipitously. Christians, knowing they were the targets, fled the town.

Two days later, Boko Haram returned and burned all the churches in Wagga and in the much larger adjoining community of Madagali. Also burned were the Church of Christ in Nigeria, Assemblies of God, and Catholic congregations, but the eight EYN churches took the brunt of the attack. Boko Haram settled in Madagali but left a small armed contingent in Wagga.

Since it was just Muslims left in Wagga, Boko Haram called all the Muslim men, "Come, let us pray together." They issued an ultimatum: "Who would like to join us?" A handful agreed to join. The rest asked for time to consider the invitation until the next day. Boko Haram immediately took nearly two hundred of them, old and young, to a large hall.

They were separated into groups of ten. The first ten were killed with an ax, the next ten killed with a cutlass, and the third group killed with a gun. Then the process was repeated over and over. One of each ten was granted "mercy" and subsequently fled. The most elderly were spared and those under fifteen were incorporated into Boko Haram to be shaped as new fighting recruits. The slaughter led some who had volunteered to reconsider and later escape.

In Wagga, the small Muslim community had prayed five times each day. They removed their shoes and washed their feet before praying as do most Muslims. Boko Haram pray just once each day, about seven in the morning, and leave their shoes on while praying.

Boko Haram did not kill the women when they came to Wagga, but took all the food from the houses, leaving nothing for the women. Sarah (not her real name) was a single-parent farmer, growing ground nuts, red and white beans, and maize. Now she was rarely able to leave her home. When she did she was required to cover her head so that neighbors could barely recognize her, or she them. The few Christian women still in Wagga made a pact with the Muslim men who remained to live together, but not as married couples, as cover from Boko Haram. Those men were able to slip away at times to grind grain for the women to eat.

Sarah was a Christian, but whether Christian or Muslim, living conditions for women were horrible. She and three other women would meet for prayer whenever the men went out. Her prayer was always, "God, how can I escape to the mountains?"

When Boko Haram first raided Wagga, Sarah had fled to safety in the mountains. She returned only when she realized her thirteen-year-old mentally challenged daughter was missing. She stayed for her daughter, who was later brutally raped by Boko Haram in the six intervening months. The population of Wagga and Madagali together has dropped to only 200 people.

The day after Christmas, Sarah awakened at 11:00 in the night and a vision told her to run for safety. She and one of her friends who agreed to join her fled to the mountain. Surprisingly they found forty-three other women and two men who had similarly fled from other places. They crossed safely into Cameroon to Mokolo village where they found some immediate assistance.

Then again as a group, they crossed the border and found refuge in Yola. From there, Sarah came to Jos where her brother has been caring for two of her young children who had escaped in July. She does not know whether her daughter is still alive, but she does praise God for the chance to again see her people.

AISHATU MARGIMA

Aishatu was born into an EYN family in Asharo Uba, Borno State, where her father was one of the first ordained EYN pastors. She remembers the visits of guests from the Church of the Brethren with names like Kulp, Royer, and Grimley. She worked as a midwife/nurse and then as director of a health center. Later she became head of the EYN HIV program that highlighted her capable skills in community organizing.

On retirement, she started an NGO, Women and Youth Empowerment for Advancement and Health Initiative. WYEAHI attracted the attention and funding of the World Bank. She has utilized that assistance to help displaced families regain economic control of their lives. Providing tools like sewing machines, draft animals and plows, and grain grinders help families begin a business. Animals and seeds provide meat and wool for sale and food and milk for the family. These income generators are supplemented by extensive training that includes record keeping, maintenance and care of machines and animals, and encouragement to save some of the income for eventual replacement of tools and animals.

Aishatu has sent a proposal to Brethren Disaster Ministries with a request for funding to provide this type of assistance to displaced families who are even now returning to Mubi, Gombe, and Hong, three of the six communities in which she has proposed working.

Her second marriage was to a Muslim man. Her work has always stressed an interfaith aspect because that is the reality in the communities with which she works. After she had married, her father lost his ordination in the local EYN congregation because he had "allowed" her to marry a Muslim. EYN headquarters reinstalled his ordination saying, "There is no rule like this in EYN."

Aishatu has an infrastructure in place to move quickly if her proposal is accepted by BDM. Her NGO is only one of several that are being considered as complementary programs to the larger relief work of the EYN Crisis Management Team.

CHIBOK DISPLACED

Several days before Christmas 2014, Boko Haram raided Chibok again. Remember that in April Boko Haram kidnapped over 300 young women in Chibok. Most of them are still missing. This time some older women and a young man were abducted.

Even though Nigerian military are reportedly still in control of the town, after the Christmas attack, families in that area fled. Today just over three weeks later, 231 people from Chibok settled in a neighborhood in the village of Pegi, outside Kuje city on one of the growing edges of Abuja. They would have had to travel two days even with an organized departure by public transportation. Terrorized flight is usually not organized.

The chief of Pegi is very understanding, saying, "We weep with those who weep." He met with trauma representatives of the EYN Crisis Management Team, EYN district leadership, and some of the Chibok community under a cool mango tree. He and the mostly Christian village are very welcoming.

The EYN team were visiting to arrange for trauma workshops in the IDP camps around Abuja. As usual, their presence was the impetus that brought people together, this time just under half of the entire displaced community. Visitors sat on benches and plastic chairs that appeared from nowhere. The rest of those gathered lounged on mats laid carefully to take advantage of the shady spots in the courtyard.

A nursing mother was laughing with other women on her mat. Tiny children were wrapped on mothers' backs and older children sat together, quietly moving around in a center mat. It seemed some of the young men must have been employed as they came in later, apparently summoned from their work.

From the courtyard, any visitor could see mud brick homes, roofed with hot metal or cool thatch. Mud grain bins in the yard were elevated on sturdy mud legs so the chickens were able to scratch for insects underneath the well-preserved grain. From an opening in the courtyard circle, the fields were easily visible, just a short distance from this compound. Around Pegi, rows and fields of two-foot high mounds were prepared for the imminent planting of yams, one of the staples in this part of Nigeria.

One person had immediately offered his compound to the visitors. In fact, he moved out entirely so that all his space could be utilized by the newcomers. Others in the area offered homes free of charge to those from Chibok. On one wall of the courtyard was the inscription "God is King."

If Jesus had been there in person he would have said, "I saw Satan fall like lightning (Luke 10:18) in the face of the joy and grace of the Chibok families and the hospitality of the Pegi community." The power of death is destroyed in simple ways.

DANIEL JOHN

Daniel has been a driver for EYN travelers since 2002. He is married with seven living children and lives with a brother, who is also married with one child. Miriam, his mother, is still living and is caring for nine other extended family members.

When Boko Haram raided EYN headquarters October 29, Daniel escaped with all his family and ended up in Jos where he continues to work as a driver with EYN. But he had fields of beans and groundnuts near Mubi ready to harvest when he fled. He does not know if loose livestock have destroyed his harvest.

Daniel's mother crossed into Cameroon for safety when Boko Haram ransacked the areas surrounding Mubi. Her group of ten has faced difficult conditions in the mountains of Cameroon because there have been no relief agencies or government assistance coming to the aid of these refugees. As returnees have reported, "We lived on leaves." The ten people in her group just returned to the Yola area and are living in the IDP camps that have dramatically increased the Yola population. Daniel was able to visit his mother one day while the group he drives for was conducting a trauma healing workshop at the Vinikilang EYN congregation in Yola.

Though some families are slowly returning to Mubi, Daniel has his job in Jos, which helps support the members of his and his brother's families. He faces a difficult choice between the income-producing job in central Nigeria and the possible harvest and extended family back in the eastern part of Nigeria. What would you do if you were in his shoes?

EYN STRUCTURE AND MEMBERSHIP

Ekklesiyar Yan'uwa a Nigeria (EYN) has fifty districts. Each district encompasses four to fifteen local congregations, for a total of 456 congregations in EYN. Congregations start two to six preaching points in the region of the congregation, which can move toward congregational status as they gain members and financial stability. There are 2,280 preaching points in EYN and they each could have 200 to 300 members. Congregations would be led by pastors with additional staff as needed. The preaching points rely on the leadership of the congregational pastor and an evangelist. Because of distance, there may be other informal gatherings of EYN members where folks gather in members' homes for prayer and singing.

How does a person become a member of EYN? The process can start when a group of people desire to move toward membership. A congregation would form a covenant class for the prospective members to study the bible and teachings of the church for three to six months, the length depending on the level of knowledge of the interested persons. At the close of that period, the prospective members would take a covenant accepting Jesus as their Lord and Savior.

At that point they would be ready to join a baptismal class for membership applicants. This would be a time for more extensive discipleship study, again for three to six months depending on the needed study. At the conclusion of that preparation period, they could be accepted as members and baptized into the church. Then they could join in the love feast and communion and be eligible to hold office in the church. They would be expected to participate fully in the life of the church, carrying out responsibilities and maintaining financial support of the church. Tithing is strongly encouraged for members.

The above description is a basic picture of EYN before the start of the disastrous attacks by Boko Haram that ignited most severely beginning in 2009. Since Boko Haram's region of operation and control mirrors the primary area of EYN membership, EYN has been devastated. Of the fifty districts, only about seven are unscathed by the violence. Congregations in most of those seven districts are hosting displaced EYN families and supporting the needs of the displaced. The violence has destroyed 278 of the churches and another 1,674 preaching points, and 356 of the 456 pastors have moved because of the danger. Admittedly, some of the congregational church buildings that have been burned have congregations that continue to meet in other spaces. Between eight and ten thousand members have been killed in the violence. As many as 600,000 of the 1,000,000 members are unaccounted for, while well over 200,000 are internally displaced within Nigeria or are refugees in neighboring countries.

What would any denomination do if faced with such a catastrophe? What would any other Christian group do if they heard about such a story? EYN has a vision to grow the church. The Church of the Brethren has heard the vision and chosen to dig very deeply to stand with and undergird the relief process of EYN. If you aren't, you are invited to do so!

GOD'S DISTRIBUTION

Three Crisis Team members traveled to Biu on Saturday to complete a relief distribution. One day earlier it had appeared as though the process might fall through. Vehicle plans were not coming together and finances seemed to be held up, even though approval for the funds had taken place a couple weeks earlier.

Our driver picked me up at eight Saturday morning. One of the two district secretaries from Biu was traveling with the Team. We stopped to pick up the other two team members as we drove out of Jos. There had been some question whether it was safe for me, a very visible white person, to travel into this region, which had experienced Boko Haram attacks at several places along the route.

The road deteriorated as we traveled through three states before reaching Borno State. The last two hours were slow because of a heavily potholed road surface. There were regular security checkpoints and occasional vigilante roadblocks to supplement government patrols. Around Gombe and as we neared Biu, there were increasing signs of the Boko Haram suicide bombings and fire attacks against checkpoint sites, police stations, a hospital, and a gas station close to an intersection with another security checkpoint.

When we arrived at the EYN #1 Biu compound, most of the supplies were already on site, delivered by a local EYN businessman the Team had called the evening before. We still did not have definite numbers for the EYN displaced families or individuals. There were some outdated pages recording IDPs, but the numbers we started hearing from the two district secretaries were much higher than we had figured because of recent attacks on EYN communities outside of Biu.

We asked congregations during their worship at the six nearby churches to announce our plans for a 1 p.m. relief distribution. All these churches were hosting IDPs in the churches or with families. When the one o'clock time arrived, the church building was packed with people and others were outside.

We had decided the night before to ask for just one representative from each family to attend the distribution. We had decided that we might only have enough supplies for one item per family—a big bag of rice, a larger bag of maize, or a box containing packages of noodles. We also had boxes of soap and we intended to give two bars to each family. To make the process smoother we made tickets, color coded and numbered, for the total supply of the three items.

With the crowds of people before us Sunday afternoon we considered providing one item for every two families. We were worried that the distribution could deteriorate quickly. Then three ideas surfaced in rapid succession: 1) We would prioritize displaced pastors; 2) Widows would also receive priority; 3) We would start handing out tickets (each family representative picked a ticket from a bag), starting with people ages sixty to seventy and keep moving down a decade until all tickets were gone. That ticket indicated which item they would receive and the order in which they could collect the item.

It meant some expectant persons would not receive one of the three food items, but it would be the younger persons who could more easily find jobs in the city to provide food. At the start, there was a mass push toward the supplies, but with local helpers we were able to make clear that the distribution would start with the order of numbers from inside the church. Inside the church was also much cooler than in the hot sun out in the courtyard.

Even with the kinks in the process and a long careful explanation to make the process clear at the beginning, over one thousand people received supplies within three hours. One serendipitous event was deciding to not hand out soap to each family. This meant that there was sufficient soap to give three bars to even the individuals who had not received a ticket and others who were waiting hopefully in the courtyard outside the church.

As the distribution proceeded, many recipients thanked us for the process and for assuring that everyone received something. It was a team effort that accomplished the distribution task. The district secretaries were key to the process. The youth brigade supplied the manpower to move food items to recipients. Local church staff provided escort and number checking for each group of ten people moving from inside the church to the warehouse distribution center. Vigilante volunteers provided security for the courtyard. And the team of three provided coordination of the process. The patience and good humor of the recipients was essential for a smooth flow during the distribution. As one of the district secretaries commented, "The process was an act of God. I was worried when I saw so many potential pitfalls in the distribution."

KULP BIBLE COLLEGE

A three-member Brethren Disaster Ministries group from the Church of the Brethren was traveling on December 11 to Abuja to observe food distributions at several displaced camps around the capital. On the trip south from Jos with several members of the Crisis Management Team, commissioned earlier by the EYN Standing Committee to oversee the multi-faceted relief program, the entire group stopped to visit Kulp Bible College (KBC).

KBC had evacuated their facilities on October 29, simultaneously with EYN leadership from their headquarters in Mubi, because of the attacks from Boko Haram. School was in session so what could the college do?

Plans moved rapidly, for five weeks later classes resumed, but on a new campus near the community of Chinka, about one and a half hours from Abuja. KBC is situated on an eighty-six-hectare plot of ground already owned by EYN and that land provides abundant space for various activities. There already is an EYN congregation worshiping on the land with two others not far away.

There are three cement block structures needing only roofs and interior finishing before faculty and staff can move into those duplexes. Another completed structure provides six ready-to-use classrooms. Other buildings are already spaces for student housing. There is an excellent water source on the land and plentiful space for gardening if students and faculty wish. Engineer Ayube Gwani of the Crisis Management Team reported, "If the funds are made available, efforts to complete these facilities can begin next Monday."

The visiting group was able to meet in one of the classrooms to interact with students. Twenty-eight of the thirty students presently on campus were there, six women and twenty-two men. A majority (eighteen) of the thirty are third-year students and the other twelve are diploma students. There are many other students, but the administration wanted to push to get those graduating immediately back into their studies. (Pastors in the US should note that new pastors with EYN serve five to eight years being mentored under an experienced pastor before they can take their own congregation.)

Even when the College is able to return to its original setting, this space provides for the expansion of rapid church leadership training and the accompanying denominational growth into other parts of this country and across Africa.

Members of the Church of the Brethren in the United States who have worked at Kulp Bible College/School would be inspired by these heroic efforts. In the face of daunting obstacles, the visionary leadership of EYN has used the disaster of displacement to carry this training facility into a new space with expanded potential to grow EYN from a more parochial setting into a vision of a global church.

MIRACLE

On October 29, a call came to Emmanuel, a member of EYN, informing him that the radical, militant group Boko Haram was possibly coming into the Mubi area where he lived. He picked up his child at school but when he returned home there were seventeen militant vehicles already in his neighborhood. He had been aware that his near neighbor had connections to Boko Haram.

Emmanuel locked the front gate, cleared the main four rooms of all furniture, and closed the car in the garage. After shooting open the front gate, militants five times took two steps into his compound then stepped out again. That delay provided time for his wife and two children to hide in the small room with the furniture, and for him to climb into a space above the ceiling of one of the main rooms.

For the next thirty-two days, Boko Haram fighters and their commanders met regularly in the room under his ceiling discussing plans for attacks in the area. "Kill all the Christians and any Muslims who assist Christians. Burn all the churches." They kept coming in groups to plan for carrying out attacks. He could hear everything they said.

The daily calls to prayer gave Emmanuel sufficient time to collect water from his neighbor's well for his family and himself and return to the ceiling space. He shared that this was a time of long, unintentional fasting.

After thirty-two days, vigilantes and military units fought Boko Haram back from Mubi, and his son from Maiduguri found him in the house. The family used their own car to escape to Yola but had to travel eight hours via the neighboring country of Cameroon, because Boko Haram still controlled roads around the cities.

The family is clear. Those thirty-two days, and the continuing safety within their vulnerable spaces, were days of miracle. Praise God for miracles! Emmanuel, God is with us! (Matt 1:23)

REV. ADAMU BELLO, EYN PASTOR

Adamu Bello was born into a Muslim family in 1959, just eight kilometers from the EYN headquarters in Mubi. He was the firstborn and recalls living near enough to an EYN congregation that he could hear the singing. He even remembers a burial sermon about lightness and darkness in that church at age ten, when he was attracted by the pastor and his way of living.

After completing his training as a teacher, he taught for six years and was married during that time.

One Saturday he had a dream, telling him, "You are needed in heaven." A rope hung from heaven to his room. He climbed and fell. He then heard, "You need to climb and trust Jesus." He reached the top, and there was a large building in the distance with an open space in between. Again trust was required, as he walked across nothing. The building was empty, and only when asked to look behind him did he see photos of many different people.

Then, only when asked to look again in the distance did he see a very small door that opened into another room. Crawling through the opening he saw that one half of this room was dark and the other half was light. On the dark side was a woman at a table with worldly pleasures. Adamu was asked to choose which side he wanted. Remembering the sermon from his childhood about light and darkness, he chose the light.

In his dream, he then saw only his photo beside the door as he departed. He was told he would accept a glass of freshly squeezed juice from another climber and be invited the next day by three of his friends to join them for inappropriate activities. The next morning when waking, it happened as in his dream.

He decided to attend the church in his town. The pastor was the one who had offered him juice on his dream return from heaven. He chose to follow Jesus that day and leave Islam. Before the service was over, his father had heard of his decision. He was disowned from his entire family.

EYN sponsored him through four years of seminary. He began his ministry as an evangelist in 1990 and became the district secretary in Maiduguri in 1992. Since then, EYN has posted him in three other congregations prior to accepting his present assignment in EYN Jos.

At one point, his father was hospitalized and needed surgery. His youngest brother approached Pastor Adamu for assistance. He consented and then invited his father to recuperate in his home. Afterward his father said, "You saved my life." From that point, even though the rest of the family continued as Muslims, he was accepted as a full member of the family.

Four times while he was pastor in Maiduguri in the early years, as Christians were being killed and churches burned, Reverend Adamu was visited by teams of Boko Haram, probably coming to kill him. Each time, he prayed with them. After prayer each time, he would ask the young men to leave with his security person out the back way so they would not be killed by police, who would have been notified when Boko Haram fighters were seen entering. "I do this because I love you," he told them.

During those years, the person who washed his car was someone he shared with regularly. He shared his concerns for the youth in Boko Haram and said even if he were a political leader, he would grant grace to Boko Haram fighters if they would agree to stop fighting. Unbeknownst to him, the car wash person was a Boko Haram commandant.

Sometime later while traveling, he and his family were stopped by a large Boko Haram contingent that surrounded them on four sides. He assumed they would all be killed. As one combatant looked in the window of the vehicle, he seemed to recognize Reverend Adamu. "You may pass. You are a good man." Expecting a spray of bullets at any time, the family drove on without incident.

Today in Jos, Reverend Adamu and his congregation have had to deal with hundreds of people displaced from their homes in northeast Nigeria. Though initially fearful of what this tsunami of people might mean, three hundred families of the congregation have taken displaced families into their homes. Sometimes hosting as many as forty extra people, the families provide them with clothing, food, and finances as needed. There are regular contributions to the hosting families, as the church attempts to lighten their burden.

This EYN pastor, Reverend Adamu Bello, is an important presence in the EYN church during these difficult times of violence with the Muslim group Boko Haram.

THE FACE OF JESUS

Mairo Gadzama and her husband Mr. Wadzangiri are EYN members and have their home in Lassa, Adamawa State. They have two married daughters and three other children. On December 2, not even one month ago, Boko Haram raided Lassa, leveling the church and destroying homes.

A militant accosted Mr. Wadzangiri as others around him were fleeing. When the fighter questioned if he were a Christian, he gave affirmation of that fact. The militant shot him in his left arm. Asked if he would renounce his faith, he refused and was shot in the other arm. As the fighters moved on, he slid down the bank of a stream hiding under some tall grasses. Since Boko Haram was still searching the area, he moved from his place of shelter, washed his wounds quickly, crossed the stream and found a home some distance away where he found refuge.

Mairo fell to the ground at one point in the shooting mayhem and heard herself surrounded by five fighters. She kept quiet and they moved on. Soon someone came close and removed the scarf she had thrown over herself. That person told her she was safe, but apparently called other militants who surrounded her. Seven were there and she feared for her life. With evening approaching, they left for some unknown reason and she fled into the darkness. Running until she came to a home she didn't know, she risked entering. It was the same place her husband had found refuge.

He always carries anointing oil, so he asked his wife to bathe his wounds in oil. They were able to move from there to a safer location in Yola. His wounds are healing nicely. Mr. Wadzangiri plans to retire next year, and his great and only hope is to see the face of Christ.

WORSHIP

On Sunday, December 14, I was in Abuja, so I joined the congregation of EYN Utako, Abuja for worship. Reverend Daniel Mbaya is the lead pastor, but many other leaders shared in the service that day.

There was a Christmas theme, so the center of the sanctuary, from which three arms stretch out to provide space for the congregation, was draped with green and red cloth in a checkered pattern. The worship leader, choir director, ushers, and some members were dressed in Santa outfits.

That joy was perhaps to offset the more somber tune that met attendees as they entered the compound, with armed police/soldiers at the entrance, where concrete barrels and firm metal gates offered barriers to any potential suicide vehicles. Other guards wanded people as they entered.

But the worship was full and joyous. Seven choirs sang several selections each. Ten babies were there for dedication with their parents. It was graduation for about three dozen women who had completed training in catering, tailoring, and soap making. Daniel's father, also a pastor, was there on the platform with him for the first time ever, probably because Biu had been sacked by Boko Haram and he and the EYN congregation there were scattered.

The sermon was based on II Corinthians 8:9, saying, "Jesus chose to become poor, though rich, so that we, though poor, might become rich." Jesus became a "chenaga"—an ant who spoke our language.

Attendance for worship the previous Sunday was 2,938. This Sunday, swelled by displaced families, the numbers must have surpassed expectations, as deacons had to go back three times to get sufficient wafers for the communion, and juice ran out several times! Yes, these are trying times for EYN, but the challenges seem to have strengthened the faith and resolve of the church.

Appendix D:
DU Strategy Brainstorm Page

- Galvanize CPT regional groups to act simultaneously on DU issues.

- Build a coalition with European groups on ending DU use globally.

- Unite with environmental groups in Colonie, NY, and Stamford, CT, on DU hazards upwind and downwind at those former DU munitions production sites.

- Work with investigative journalist Seymour Hersh, Jeremy Scahill of the *Nation, Defense Monitor*, and Scott Peterson of the *Christian Science Monitor* to publicize DU problems.

- Write DU brochures for handouts.

- Set up a website for the DU campaign.

- Develop a list of suggested spiritual disciplines for those involved in the campaign.

- Put together guidelines for nonviolent action that would be signed as a commitment by participants.

- Organize sit-ins at congressional offices to remind legislators of their responsibility for DU and its consequences.

- Call for Veterans Administration hospitals, regional hospitals, and support clinics to publicize their data on DU-impacted veterans.

- Find Anthony Principi and VA spokespersons to speak on talk shows.

- Build concerted effort to get letters to the editor and discussion building in newspapers across the country.

- Billboard the DU issues.

- Organize house meetings in the communities around Jonesborough and Rocket City, two facility locations in the present production chain of DU weapons.

- Hold public prayer vigils for the victims of DU.

- Schedule public forums with representatives from the Department of Defense, healthcare field, veterans, religious community, and environmental groups.

- Get religious bodies to pass resolutions that urge *action* by members against DU.

- Call for a military boycott of handling/using DU weapons.

- Form state committees to pass legislation requiring DU testing of returning veterans. Write governors.

- Gather a team to monitor trucks in and out of Jonesborough, Rocket City, and other DU plants.

- Train civil disobedience teams to peacefully block entrances of DU plants.

- Recruit persons to push governors of Tennessee and West Virginia to develop alternatives to DU jobs.

- Call on local and regional church groups to encourage members to stop working DU jobs and help them find alternative employment.

- Build strike plans among unions against DU employment. Especially work with the steelworkers union.

- Gather medical personnel to document genetic and cancer problems among Iraq and Afghanistan veterans.

- Urge pastors to preach sermons on DU.

- Influence boards of directors of DU companies.

- Follow DU companies on the New York Stock Exchange.

- Find an ally in John Murtha, US Representative from PA and Marine Corps officer, retired from Vietnam, who was raising serious questions about use of DU munitions.

- Facilitate the process for Barbara Kingsolver or Starhawk to write their next book on DU.

- Write congressional representatives with DU questions and encourage their support of Rep. Jim McDermott's bill requiring testing of veterans for DU exposure and ending DU use until it has been proven safe.

- Build alliances with Code Pink, an activist women's group.

- Connect with coal miners and get them in the DU campaign.

- Prepare a sacrificial "first wave" of volunteers ready to risk any dangers nonviolently.

- Learn more about zeolite, an anti-radioactive material found in Black Hills, SD.

- Write district executives to obtain a list of Church of the Brethren/ Mennonite churches in campaign areas.

- Grow a list of volunteers ready to be members of the permanent campaign team.

- Have all Camp Casey folks (address lists) write Congress, President, VA, and letters to the editor about DU.

- Do prison orientation and preparation in the event of arrests.

- What if there is a major violent clampdown by security forces against the nonviolent DU campaign?

- Get the *Defense Monitor* and *Washington Spectator* to do exclusive issues on Depleted Uranium.

- Who will we attract to be the nonviolent training units?

- Does the campaign require a full-time presence, a full-time team?

- How do we maintain the initiative?

- Who are the other individuals and groups with which we can build alliances? Contact information?

Further Suggested Reading

Ackerman, Peter and Jack Duvall. *A Force More Powerful: A Century of Nonviolent Conflict*. New York: St. Martin's, 2000. *Good on strategy and campaign vision.*

Alison, James, O.P. *Knowing Jesus*. Springfield: Templegate, 1994. *Resurrection precedes and inspires the New Testament, especially the gospels.*

Auckerman, Dale. *Darkening Valley: a Biblical Perspective on Nuclear War*. New York: Seabury, 1981. *Powerful depth! Impotence of the powers of death in the eyes of God.*

Bailie, Gil. *Violence Unveiled: Humanity at the Crossroads*. New York, Crossroad, 1995. *Jesus exposed the scapegoat myth, and resurrection offers a way out of this crisis of violence.*

Barbé, Dominique. *Theology of Conflict*. Maryknoll: Orbis, 1989. *Develops René Girard's mimetic violence and a good chapter on fasting.*

Barrett, Greg. *The Gospel of Rutba*. Maryknoll: Orbis, 2012. *Good Samaritan story on Iraqi highway for CPT and Voices.*

Bass, Diana Butler. *A People's History of Christianity*. New York: Harper One: 2009. *Little-known stories, many women activists, and Rutba story.*

Brown, Tricia, ed. *118 Days: Christian Peacemaker Teams Held Hostage in Iraq*. Chicago: CPT, 2008. *28 writers on the CPT hostage crisis.*

————. *Getting in the Way: Stories from Christian Peacemaker Teams*. Scottdale: Herald, 2005. *Creative stories of nonviolence.*

Budde, Michael. *The (Magic) Kingdom of God: Christianity and Global Culture Industries*. Boulder: Westview, 1997. *San Egidio Community and the forming of church communities that create God's new world.*

Burrowes, Robert. *The Strategy of Nonviolent Defense: A Gandhian Approach*. Albany: State University of New York Press, 1996. *Nonviolent strategy based on decreasing the power of the opponent and increasing the power of the resistance. Good practical read.*

Carretto, Carlo. *The Desert in the City*. Cleveland: Collins, 1979. *You shall not escape from love.*

Coates, Ta-Nehisi. *Between the World and Me*. New York: Spiegel and Grou, 2018. *Letter to his son that serves as a ladder of hope.*

Cone, James H. *The Cross and the Lynching Tree*. Maryknoll: Orbis, 2011. *The tree that destroys both Black and white and the symbol that offers a Way through the alienation.*

Dear, John. *Peace Behind Bars: A Peacemaking Priest's Journal from Jail.* Franklin: Sheed & Ward, 1999. *Social change comes from willingness to suffer.*

Désroches, Leonard. *Allow the Water: Anger, Fear, Power, Work, Sexuality, Community and the Spirituality and Practices of Nonviolence.* Toronto: Dunamis, 1996. *Kitchen table theology from personal experience.*

Diamond, Jared. *Guns, Germs and Steel; the Fates of Human Societies.* New York: W.W. Norton and Co., 1999. *His thesis offers an answer to why Pizarro conquered the Incas instead of the reverse.*

Dolci, Danilo. *The Man Who Plays Alone.* London: Anchor, 1970. *Sicilian Gandhi.*

———. *Outlaws.* New York: Orion, 1961. *Reverse strike and community organizing in the face of structures that murder the poor.*

Douglas, Kelly Brown. *Stand Your Ground: Black Bodies and the Justice of God.* Maryknoll: Orbis, 2015. *Powerful theology with a moral imagination that opens the crucified to a resurrection lived out in today's reality.*

Douglass, James. *JFK and the Unspeakable: Why He Died and Why It Matters.* Maryknoll: Orbis. 2008. *The unspeakable survives when fearful people provide it cover, but anyone can turn.*

Easwaran, Ekneth. *A Man to Match His Mountains, Badshah Khan, Nonviolent Soldier of Islam.* Tomales: Nilgiri, 1999. *Most powerful story of a nonviolent army and its leader. CPT passed out the book in Gaza and Iraq.*

Ferner, Mike. *Inside the Red Zone: A Veteran for Peace Reports from Iraq.* Westport: Praeger, 2006. *Pictures of CPT and Voices with words and camera from Iraq.*

Friesen, Dorothy. *Critical Choices: A Journey with the Filipino People.* Grand Rapids: Eerdmans, 1988. *Can we make the hard long term commitment needed for the justice struggle?*

Friesen, Dorothy and Marilyn Abesamis, eds. *Create Space for Peace: Forty Years of Peacemaking, Gene Stoltzfus, 1940–2010.* Deerfield Beach: Tri Mark, 2010. *Letters, papers and blogs by Gene, first CPT director, to encourage peace travelers.*

Froemming, David. *Salvation Story.* Eugene: Resource, 2016. *Biblical commentary— how the Jesus story saves us from imitating violence (René Girard) to instead imitate the servant, Prince of Peace, Jesus.*

Giono, Jean. *The Man Who Planted Trees.* Chelsea: Chelsea Green. 1985. *A story of perseverance and hope that transforms a wind-swept, drought seared land.*

Gish, Art. *At-Tuwani Journal: Hope and Nonviolent Action in a Palestinian Village.* Scottdale: Herald, 2008. *Stories from the Way.*

———. *Hebron Journal: Stories of Nonviolent Peacemaking.* Scottdale: Herald, 2001. *Stories and reflections from the West Bank to train peacemakers.*

———. *Muslim, Christian, Jew: The Oneness of God and the Unity of Our Faith. . . a Personal Journey in Three Abrahamic Religions.* Eugene: Wipf and Stock, 2012. *What unites and divides these faiths? Can one, Art, be adherent of all three?*

Gish, Peggy. *Iraq: A Journey of Hope and Peace.* Scottdale: Herald, 2004. *Stories from CPT in Iraq from 2002–2005.*

———. *Walking through Fire: Iraqi's Struggle for Justice and Reconciliation.* Eugene: Wipf and Stock, 2013. *Stories and analysis from CPT in Iraq, 2005–2011.*

Griffith, Lee. *The Fall of the Prison: Biblical Perspectives on Prison Abolition.* Grand Rapids: Eerdmans, 1993. *Discipleship seeking to live out this fall.*

———. *God Is Subversive: Talking Peace in a Time of Empire.* Grand Rapids: Eerdmans, 2011. *If I had read this before writing my book, Lee, I might not have been in such a rush!*

———. *The War on Terrorism and the Terror of God.* Grand Rapids: Eerdmans, 2002. *God's tools and perspective far above the "Shock and Awe" yet to happen.*

Kellerman, Bill Wylie. *Principalities in Particular: A Practical Theology of the Powers that Be.* Minneapolis: Fortress, 2017. *A theology with feet that confronts the angels of injustice and violence.*

———. *Seasons of Faith and Conscience: Kairos, Confession, Liturgy.* Maryknoll: Orbis, 1991. *The Kingdom of Jesus' lordship develops the opposition to the demonic nature of the kingdom's powers and principalities.*

Kern, Kathleen. *In Harm's Way: A History of Christian Peacemaker Teams.* Portland: Cascadia, 2009. *Detailed, documented description of the flow of CPT from movement to institution.*

Kimmerer, Robin Wall. *Braiding Sweetgrass: Indigenous Wisdom, Scientific Knowledge and the Teaching of Plants.* Minneapolis: Milkweed Editions, 2013. *Crafted wonder. Collateral damage. Then restoration.*

Loney, James. *Captivity: 118 Days in Iraq and the Struggle for a World without War.* Toronto: Alfred A. Knopf, 2011. *Four CPTers kidnapped, irony of release and yet, transformation.*

Longacre, Doris Jansen. *More-With-Less Cookbook.* Scottdale: Herald, 1976. *Introduction on changing by eating lower on the food chain.*

McManus, Philip and Gerald Schlabach. *Relentless Persistence: Nonviolent Action in Latin America.* Santa Cruz: New Society, 1992. *Humanization of nonviolence and creating the new reality alongside resistance.*

Preston Smith, Joel. *Night of a Thousand Stars and Other Portraits of Iraq.* Tuscon: Nazraeli, 2006. *A photographic glimpse of Iraq in the midst of war.*

Roche, Douglas. *Beyond Hiroshima.* Ottawa: Novalis, 2005. *Nuclear non-proliferation agreement requires nuclear powers to de-nuke.*

Sharp, Gene. *The Politics of Nonviolent Action.* Boston: Porter Sargent, 1973. *Voluntary obedience is all that sustains power, but nonviolence decentralizes power. Excellent stimulating stories from history. Basic source.*

Silone, Ignazio. *Bread and Wine.* New York: New American Library, 1963. *A small, single "No" in the face of injustice can topple that disorder, and how can you silence a cadaver?*

Solzhenitsyn, Aleksandr. *The Cancer Ward.* New York: Dell, 1973. *Quotes Pushkin: "[Our] choice is but to be tyrant, traitor, prisoner. No other choice. . ."*

Thurman, Howard. *Jesus and the Disinherited.* Boston: Beacon, 1976. *God's love of each one empowers even love in the face of the injustice and hate of those who have falsely read justification into Christian structures.*

Tolstoy, Leo. *The Law of Love and the Law of Violence.* Chicago: Holt, Rinehart and Winston, 1970. *Law of love condemns any order founded on violence and that law has no exception for Christians.*

Wink, Walter. *Engaging the Powers: Discernment and Resistance in a World of Domination.* Minneapolis: Fortress, 1992. *God's domination-free order forces out sexism, racism, materialism, violence, and environmental destruction. This is a nonviolence handbook.*

Zahn, Gordon. *In Solitary Witness: The Life and Death of Franz Jägerstatter*. Chicago: Holt, Rinehart and Winston, 1964. *A lone Austrian peasant who refused to fight in the German army and was executed by the Nazis.*

Zinn, Howard. *A People's History of the United States*. New York: Harper and Row, 1980. *A history of the oppressed, minorities, and those working for change.*